myparty

my**party**

canapés and cocktails
pete evans

cocktails by mark ward

MURDOCH BOOKS

contents

my party

I love to throw a party. Over the past 20 years I have catered for all types of people, from royalty and the rich and famous, to the very demanding aspects of organising my daughters' birthday parties and everyone in between. I find catering for parties an exhilarating and rewarding experience as you can be up close and personal with your guests and it's a lot more interactive than a dinner party.

During this time, I have picked up a lot of handy tips to make sure that whatever you serve, it will be the hit of the party and not cause too much stress in the kitchen. Here are some of my simple rules for success:

- The food shouldn't be too big to fit in your guests' mouths — it should only be one or two bites at most, otherwise you will need to serve it in its own bowl or plate.
- Different platters are fun to play around with, as are different serving glasses and cups for wet dishes such as soups and desserts.
- Some of my favourite ways to serve tasty party morsels are on toasted croutons, fried wontons, witlof leaves, cucumber slices, sushi rice, puff pastry, lettuce cups, potato crisps or oyster and scallop shells.
- As often as possible, all the prep should be done in advance, so when your guests arrive you just need to assemble. It's always good to get some extra hands involved, especially the kids, as they love to stack things on top of each other and because they have smaller fingers, they often do a neater job of it than we do.
- Having a theme in place for your party generally makes life a lot easier. Not only the drinks but also the food can follow a particular theme.

My Party has been divided into eight chapters that define my style of entertaining and give a great overview of some themes you can use for your next party.

pool party

I grew up on the water and still live on the coast so a pool party for me is a no-brainer. These days we are all embracing the whole taking-the-indoors-outdoors concept with many adapting their homes and kitchens to be able to enjoy entertaining outside. What's better than being poolside with an ice-cold drink in one hand and a tasty morsel in the other? Most of these recipes are cold preparations that can be made in advance, then simply placed on trays and served. Mark Ward, the genius behind the cocktails in this book, has created an interesting array of new drinks to enjoy but also kept in a few old-school favourites so we can reminisce. If drinking and swimming is not your thing, all the drinks can be adapted to create mocktails — just lose the booze and increase the fruit for an equally satisfying refreshment.

club med

The Mediterranean encompasses so many diverse flavours, from Italy right through to Turkey. I could write a book on these alone. The greatest thing about the region is that seasonal produce is truly the star. As a chef, just showcasing the diversity of this region and the many cultures it contains within a relatively small area is mind-blowing. Think ancient rows of olive trees, the freshest seafood, figs with buffalo mozzarella, does it get any better? Mark's drinks can be for any time of day and so can the food, let the seasons be your ultimate guide.

spice nights

Asian cuisine is special and linked intrinsically to culture and lifestyle. Bites bursting with sour, salt, spice and lime lend themselves perfectly to a canapé adaptation, it's all about balance and seasoning. Generally the Asian climates are hot and humid so a refreshing, icy cocktail is the perfect partner for this type of food. Take a trip to Chinatown and invest in some key Asian groceries, for example, palm sugar, betel leaves and exotic fruit, then experiment with ideas and flavours based on your personal taste. If you don't have a blender for Mark's cocktails, just use a mortar and pestle for a similar result. The drinks Mark has created for this chapter are predominantly fruit-based with lots of ice and the occasional splash of whisky. You will find it's hard and very expensive to buy any type of wine in Asia, it's just not their thing. For tropical and warm climates of Asia or anytime here at home, if all else fails, just serve with chilled beer. Easy!

carnival

I believe South and Central American food will be a huge culinary force in the coming decade — the use of spice and fresh produce works so well with entertaining — the flavours are deliciously addictive. The respect given to the ingredients used in the cuisine is wonderful, as too are the drinks. This chapter features cocktails ranging from the heat of Mexico, using high-end 100% agave tequila, to drinks made with Mezcal for smoky South American nights. South of Mexico is a continent of diverse cultures and our chilli martini reflects this, heart and soul.

supper club

Supper clubs are becoming increasingly popular and that's a good thing. In this chapter, I have created slightly more substantial versions of the canapé to be served midway through your party to help line the stomach. We find with our catering that people are looking for canapés to start but can become ravenous again after 9.30 pm. I highly recommend these dishes as perfect midnight hunger-buster options. Each and every drink featured here holds a story and element of elegance only truly appreciated at night. This chapter contains cocktails for discerning drinkers who wish to explore a range of flavours and classic cocktail combinations. These are the ultimate drinks for suave, ambassadorial-style moments while entertaining at home.

chill factor

As the weather cools we like to find comfort in our meals just as much as from our knitted socks and woollen blankets. In this chapter, I've included some great winter warmer recipes and Mark offers some equally comforting drinks to heat the back of your throat, structured around warming notes, or dark spirits and winter fruit. Warm yourself by an open fire in a ski chalet or your own cosy lounge with spicy mulled wine or a bourbon toddy. This truly is food for the soul.

black tie

To become a professional chef we undertake a four-year apprenticeship, which means long hard hours spent in a kitchen training and learning from your peers. And that is just the beginning; you never stop learning and being inspired. This chapter allows me to showcase the more technical side of cooking by pulling out some slightly more difficult manoeuvres with spectacular results. Creating a comfortable ambience for your guests can be just as important as the food and the drinks you serve at any event, big or small. Black tie means it's time to pull out the best cutlery and crockery, polish up those glasses and throw away the paper napkins. As for the drinks, it's everything to do with signature touches: the tailored ice, rare-release spirits and unique ingredients. It doesn't matter if it's your anniversary, the in-laws are visiting or you're simply out to treat yourself, there's something for the entertaining king, queen, prince or princess in this section.

high tea

My pastry chef, Monica, has helped me create this chapter – she has a real talent and eye for all things sweet. As Mark has shown with his drink selection, desserts and cocktails can sometimes be almost one and the same as they share common ingredient bases such as chocolate, coffee and flavoured liqueurs. The perfect end to any party has to be an espresso martini with a tiramisù.

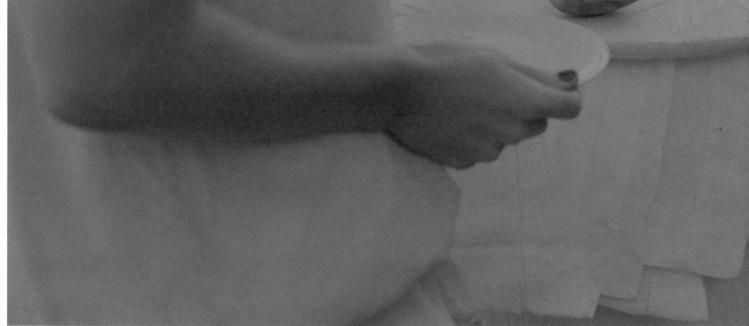

pool party

I grew up on the water and still live on the coast so the pool party for me is a no-brainer. These days we are all embracing the concept of taking the indoors outdoors with many adapting their homes and kitchens to be able to enjoy entertaining outside. What's better than being poolside with an ice-cold drink in one hand and a tasty morsel in the other?

One of the most famous salads in the world and the first one I learned to make at culinary school was the Caesar salad. I couldn't tell you how many ways I have made this over the years or how many different ways I've been presented with it while dining. It's one of my favourite salads to eat and I love ordering it to see the chefs' interpretations. But this book is about canapés and how to serve them – in a glass looks funky but I think served in a tart-shaped crouton topped with a quail egg is perfect – you may have to pre-order your quail eggs from the butcher, otherwise, just boil some normal eggs and chop them finely.

caesar salad tartlets with quail eggs

MAKES 20

20 slices white or wholemeal bread
100 ml (3½ fl oz) melted butter
5 quail eggs
white vinegar
6 bacon slices, cut into lardons
1 small cos (romaine) lettuce
100 g (3½ oz/1 cup) grated parmesan, plus extra to serve

caesar dressing
4 free-range egg yolks
1 small garlic clove, chopped
2 teaspoons dijon mustard
2 tablespoons lemon juice
2 tablespoons white wine vinegar
5 anchovies, finely chopped
200 ml (7 fl oz) olive oil
200 ml (7 fl oz) vegetable oil

Preheat the oven to 160°C (315°F/Gas 2–3). Remove the crusts from the slices of bread. Using a rolling pin, roll out the bread slices to 5 mm (¼ inch) thick. Cut out circles using a 7 cm (2¾ inch) diameter round cutter, brush with some butter and press into greased mini-muffin tin holes to form a crouton tart. Place in the oven and bake for 5–10 minutes or until they are golden.

To make the Caesar dressing, place the egg yolks, garlic, mustard, lemon juice, white wine vinegar and anchovy in a jug and with a hand-held blender, start blending. Add in the combined oils slowly until creamy, season with salt and pepper.

Place the quail eggs in a saucepan, cover with cold water and add a splash of white vinegar. Bring them to the boil, then remove from the heat immediately. Cool the eggs under cold running water, then peel and cut into quarters.

Fry the bacon in a large frying pan over high heat until crispy. Remove to a plate lined with kitchen paper to drain and cool.

Just before serving, finely shred the lettuce and dress with a small amount of the Caesar dressing. Add the parmesan then fill the tart shells to just below the top. Place a quail egg quarter on the top of each and finish with a sprinkle of bacon, sea salt, a drizzle of the Caesar dressing and some extra grated parmesan.

I am most happy when I am sitting in a great Japanese restaurant at the sushi bar and I can see what the chef is preparing in front of me — I tend to become mesmerised watching them meticulously slice the fish. There's no excuse for eating badly made sushi when it's so easy to prepare yourself.

pete's sushi and tempura shiitake

MAKES 48 PIECES

To make the sushi rice, cook the rice with 330 ml (11¼ fl oz/1⅓ cups) water following packet instructions.

Meanwhile, stir the sugar, salt and vinegar in a small saucepan over low heat until the sugar and salt dissolves.

Spread the hot, cooked rice on a large tray and sprinkle over the rice vinegar dressing. Stir with chopsticks or a fork to cool and distribute the dressing evenly (see note). Press the rice into 24 blocks, each about 5 cm (2 inches) long and 2 cm (¾ inch) wide. Cover the rice with a damp cloth as you work.

Spread 16 of the rice blocks with wasabi. Place a wire rack over a naked flame and once hot, lay the salmon and kingfish on the rack until it gets lightly charred marks but is still raw. Cook on one side only. Place the raw side of the fish pieces down on the rice blocks. Squeeze some lemon juice over the fish and season with a little sea salt.

To make the cuttlefish sushi, top the remaining 8 rice blocks with the lemon zest and shiso. Score the top side of the cuttlefish with a sharp knife, making shallow incisions lengthways. Lay the raw scored cuttlefish on the rice blocks. Sprinkle with the toasted sesame seeds, if using and a little sea salt. Serve with soy sauce if desired.

To make the tempura shiitake, put the flour in a mixing bowl and slowly whisk in the cold mineral water, until the batter is the consistency of pouring cream.

Heat the oil to 180°C (350°F) in a wok or deep saucepan. Dip the mushrooms into the tempura batter and deep-fry in batches until golden and crispy. Drain on kitchen paper, cut in half with a sharp knife and season with sea salt and a squeeze of lemon juice.

NOTE: Sushi rice is best when not refrigerated and used within 2 hours of making. However, if you like, you could shape the rice into blocks, place in airtight containers and refrigerate for up to 12 hours, then bring back to room temperature for 1 hour before finishing.

sushi rice
210 g (7½ oz/1 cup) sushi rice
2 tablespoons sugar
1 teaspoon sea salt
2 tablespoons rice vinegar (or ponzu flavoured vinegar)

seared salmon and kingfish belly
2 teaspoons wasabi paste
8 x 20 g (¾ oz) slices of salmon belly
8 x 20 g (¾ oz) slices of kingfish belly
juice of ½ lemon

cuttlefish with lemon and shiso leaf
zest of 1 lemon
8 torn shiso leaves or baby shiso leaves plus extra to serve
8 x 20 g (¾ oz) pieces of cleaned cuttlefish
1 teaspoon of toasted mixed white and black sesame seeds (optional)
sea salt
soy sauce, to serve (optional)

tempura shiitake
200 g (7 oz) tempura flour (available at Asian grocers)
350 ml (12 fl oz) cold sparkling mineral water
peanut oil, for deep-frying
12 shiitake mushrooms, stems trimmed
juice of 1 lemon

One of my favourite destinations is Darwin. Something about the heat when you get off the plane and the sheer laid-back nature of the town is comforting to me. I get the same feeling each time I visit. On one of my last trips I was fortunate enough to do some filming with one of the locals, Lynette Ainsworth. This is one of her recipes learned during her time in another tropical paradise ... Tahiti. It's a beautiful dish and one I urge you to serve at your next party — especially if the weather is hot!

tahitian fish salad

SERVES 20

600 g (1 lb 5 oz) fresh fish such as barramundi, tuna or mahi mahi, skin removed and discarded and flesh cut into small cubes
2 garlic cloves, crushed
juice of 6 limes
1 tablespoon chopped coriander (cilantro) leaves
1 red chilli, finely diced
400 ml (14 fl oz) coconut milk
1 tablespoon red wine vinegar
2 drops Tabasco
2 carrots, grated
2 tomatoes, finely diced
½ red capsicum (pepper), finely diced
4 spring onions (scallions), finely sliced

Combine the fish, garlic, lime juice, coriander and chilli in a non-reactive bowl and refrigerate for 5 minutes.

Meanwhile, make a dressing by combining the coconut milk, red wine vinegar, some salt and pepper and the Tabasco.

Drain the fish, pour over the dressing and add the carrot, tomato, and capsicum. Serve in small bowls and sprinkle with the onion.

Jacinta Cannataci is my head chef at Hugos Bar Pizza and one-half of the Cannataci twins. Monica, her sister, is my pastry chef. The girls have been working with me for about six years now and I may be the luckiest restaurateur in the world to have them with me. This tuna tartare recipe is one of Jacinta's. It's a great one because it is simple to make but looks like a lot of work has gone into creating it.

tuna tartare on potato crisp

MAKES 20

To make the potato crisps, thinly slice the potatoes on a mandolin, wash in cold water to remove some of the starch and pat dry with kitchen paper. Heat the oil to 160°C (315°F) in a wok or deep saucepan, fry the potato slices on both sides until light golden, drain on kitchen paper and sprinkle with sea salt.

To make the tomato chutney, heat the olive oil in a saucepan over medium heat, add the mustard seeds and onion and cook until lightly brown. Add the garlic, chilli, ginger and turmeric and cook until fragrant. Add the tomato and cook until softened then add the red wine vinegar and sugar. Cook until the liquid has reduced by half. Season with salt and pepper and cool.

Dice the tuna into small pieces and place in a chilled bowl. Finely chop 3 of the green beans, add to the tuna with 3 tablespoons of the tomato chutney, the olives and basil and mix until combined. Season with salt and pepper.

Spoon a teaspoon of the tuna mix on a potato crisp, finely slice the remaining green beans on an angle and sprinkle over the top.

200 g (7 oz) best-quality sashimi
 (tuna, salmon or kingfish)
5 green beans, blanched
50 g (1¾ oz) dried kalamata olives, diced
4 basil leaves, finely shredded

potato crisps
4 kipfler potatoes, peeled
vegetable oil for deep-frying

tomato chutney
1 tablespoon extra virgin olive oil
1 tablespoon yellow mustard seeds
1 onion, chopped
3 garlic cloves, chopped
1 long red chilli, chopped
1 tablespoon ground ginger
1 tablespoon ground turmeric
6 vine-ripened tomatoes, diced
50 ml (1½ fl oz) red wine vinegar
50 g (1¾ oz) sugar

One of the highlights of any party is being presented with mini sandwiches. There is something very comforting about them. They remind me of my childhood when I used to ask Mum to cut the crusts off for me. These days, I love the crust but whenever I'm catering I remove them as they are more attractive that way. Here are two grown-up versions of the humble finger sandwich — if roast chicken and pork aren't exciting enough for you then try some of my other favourite ingredients such as crabmeat, freshly cooked prawns, lobster medallions, scampi, sea urchin and deep-fried oysters.

roasted chicken finger sandwiches with celeriac remoulade

MAKES 20

Combine the chicken with the mayonnaise, roasted garlic and mustard. Fold through the celeriac and season with salt and pepper.

Using a 5 cm (2 inch) round cutter cut 2 circles from each slice of bread. Butter the bread and divide the chicken mixture between 20 rounds of bread, sprinkle with chervil, top with the remaining bread rounds and serve.

2 cooked chicken breasts (or you could use leftover roast chicken), shredded
4 tablespoons good-quality whole-egg mayonnaise or aïoli
4 roasted garlic cloves, finely chopped (see page 132)
2 teaspoons wholegrain mustard
½ celeriac peeled, washed, finely sliced
20 slices fresh rye bread
softened butter
½ bunch chervil, trimmed

pork sandwiches with asian herbs and sambal

MAKES 24

Butter the bread and top 8 of the slices with the roast pork. Combine the mayonnaise and sambal and spread over the pork. Season with salt and pepper. Combine the herbs and sprinkle over the mayonnaise. Top with the remaining bread slices. Remove the crusts with a sharp knife, cut each sandwich into 3 even fingers and serve.

softened butter
16 slices white bread
200 g (7 oz) sliced roast pork (I like to use leftover roast pork)
3 tablespoons good-quality whole-egg mayonnaise
2 teaspoons good-quality sambal
1 handful of Vietnamese mint, torn
1 handful of coriander (cilantro) leaves
1 handful of Thai basil leaves, torn

There is a beautiful location in the Northern Territory that has amazing fishing and wildlife called Seven Spirit Bay. I was fortunate enough to get a guernsey a few years ago to do a spot of fishing and filming there and spent a few days with the head chef, Luke Smith. After a few beers I was treated to some of his incredible food — watermelon and feta salad — what a dish and so perfect for that climate or wherever the weather is warm.

watermelon and feta salad

MAKES 20

50 ml (1½ fl oz) balsamic vinegar
20 orange segments, excess
  juice reserved
½ small watermelon (seedless are good
  but I think seeded watermelons have a
  sweeter flavour)
200 g (7 oz) feta
20 green beans, trimmed and blanched
  and cut in half on the angle
1 handful of small basil leaves

pickled onion

100 ml (3½ fl oz) white vinegar
150 g (5½ oz) caster (superfine) sugar
½ red onion, thinly sliced

To make the pickled onion, bring the vinegar and sugar to the boil in a small saucepan. Remove from the heat and then add the red onion. Allow to cool completely.

Make a dressing with the balsamic vinegar and any juice left over from the oranges. Bring to the boil in a very small saucepan and simmer gently until slightly thickened. (Of course, if using really good balsamic, I wouldn't do this because really good balsamic is just awesome as it is!) Allow to cool completely. Slice the watermelon into rounds as thick as your finger. If you're using a seedless watermelon this bit is easy but if not just carefully pick out as many seeds as possible. Cut the watermelon rounds into small wedges, trimming away the rind. Break the feta into small squares. Place the melon in small bowls with the feta, orange segments, green beans and basil leaves. Finish off with a few slices of pickled onion and dress with a few drops of the reduced balsamic dressing.

I have served this dish as an entrée on my menu at Hugos Manly since it opened. It actually started off as a more complicated dish but after serving close to 1000 people on the first day, I desperately needed to simplify the food I served or myself and my kitchen team were going to be in a world of pain. The scallop dish needed to be a one-pan wonder so that once I had seared the scallops and placed them back in their shells, I could just make a simple dressing in the same pan and spoon it over the scallops. This was the resulting dish and it is actually much better than the original. I now serve it at every function I do.

seared scallops with tomato and basil dressing

SERVES 20

Make sure your scallops are close to room temperature before cooking (they shouldn't be cold as you will be eating them rare). Remove the scallops from their shells and set aside.

To make the dressing, gently warm the olive oil in a saucepan. Remove from the heat and mix in the lemon juice and crushed coriander seeds and leave for 1 minute. Add the basil and tomato and season with salt and pepper.

If using a barbecue, preheat to hot. Toss the scallops in the oil and season lightly with sea salt and white pepper. Cook the scallops on the barbecue, or in a frying pan over high heat, for about 30 seconds on each side so they are cooked rare. Put the scallops back on their shells and spoon over the dressing.

20 scallops on the half shell
1 tablespoon extra virgin olive oil

dressing
80 ml (2½ fl oz/⅓ cup) extra virgin olive oil
1 tablespoon lemon juice
1 teaspoon roasted coriander seeds, crushed
8 basil leaves, very finely sliced or 1 handful of small basil leaves
2 ripe tomatoes, peeled, seeded and diced

I was lucky enough to cook in the Emirates marquee at Australia's biggest horse-racing event, the Melbourne Cup. We had a beautiful Indian-inspired menu to accompany the Bollywood dancers and Indian music. We served about 25 different delicacies that day but this was simply a standout. I've amended the recipe to take out the Indian spice, but if you feel like it, just add some toasted mustard seeds and a bit of turmeric powder to the crab mix. And speaking of luck, something must have gone right as I backed the winner.

chilled pea soup with spanner crab

SERVES 20

30 g (1 oz) butter

6 spring onions (scallions), white part only, thinly sliced

310 g (11 oz/2 cups) fresh or frozen green peas

625 ml (21½ fl oz/2½ cups) chicken stock

80 g (2¾ oz/⅓ cup) crème fraîche

3 teaspoons each of finely chopped tarragon, flat-leaf (Italian) parsley and mint

200 g (7 oz) picked spanner crabmeat

Melt the butter over medium heat in a heavy-based saucepan. Add the green onions and sprinkle generously with sea salt. Cook, stirring often, for 5–7 minutes or until the onion is softened.

Stir in the peas, then the stock. Bring to a boil, reduce the heat and simmer for 15–20 minutes or until the peas are soft. While the peas are cooking, mix the crème fraîche with the tarragon, parsley and mint in a small bowl. Set aside.

When the peas are very soft, remove the saucepan from the heat and purée the contents in a blender. Press the purée through a coarse strainer into a large bowl. Thoroughly whisk in the herbed crème fraîche. Season with salt and freshly ground black pepper to taste. Chill before serving.

Chill 20 small glasses then pour in 30 ml (1 fl oz) of the pea soup and serve topped with some picked crabmeat.

Yum is pretty much all that needs to be said about these tasty treats. If you feel like it, try making your own sweet chilli sauce, it isn't very hard to do and I reckon it tastes better than the ones you buy off the supermarket shelves. You can substitute the prawns in the filling for crabmeat, fish, scallops, bug meat, lobster or even pork and chicken. Try serving it with different sauces as well — one of my favourites is hot English mustard, but be careful as it packs a punch.

fried prawn won tons with sweet chilli

MAKES 40

To make the sweet chilli sauce, dissolve the sugar and 2 tablespoons of water in a small saucepan over low heat. Cook for a further 10 minutes until the bubbles on the surface become large. Do not allow it to change colour.

Blend the chilli, garlic, galangal and sea salt. Then add to the sugar mixture along with the rice wine vinegar, cook for another 10 minutes and remove from the heat. Add the lime leaves when the sauce is cool.

Season the minced prawn with the sea salt and cracked white pepper. Add the garlic chives, lemon zest and mix well.

Lay the won ton wrappers on a work surface and fill each with a teaspoon of the prawn mixture. Brush a little of the egg around the edge of the wrapper. Join the 4 corners together and give a little twist to seal.

Heat the oil to 180°C (350°F) in a wok or deep saucepan. Fry the won tons for 2–3 minutes or until golden and crispy. Drain on kitchen paper, arrange the wontons on a platter and serve immediately with the sweet chilli sauce on the side.

400 g (14 oz) raw prawn (shrimp) meat, finely minced
sea salt
cracked white pepper
1 teaspoon chopped garlic chives
zest of 1 lemon
40 won ton wrappers
1 free-range egg, beaten
peanut oil for deep-frying
sweet chilli sauce, to serve (see below)

sweet chilli sauce
200 g (7 oz) caster (superfine) sugar
4 long red chillies, chopped
5 garlic cloves
10 g (¼ oz) fresh galangal, chopped
2½ teaspoons sea salt
100 ml (3½ fl oz) rice vinegar
3 kaffir lime leaves

poolside punch

SERVES 4

200 ml (7 fl oz) aged rum (Pampero Anejo
    Especial works well)
100 ml (3½ fl oz) lime juice
40 ml (1¼ fl oz) honey water (see page 238)
40 ml (1¼ fl oz) homemade falernum
    (see page 238)
homemade ginger beer (see page 244)
4 mint sprigs, lemon and orange wedges,
    to garnish

Place all the ingredients, except the ginger beer, in a shaker and shake over ice. Strain into four highball glasses filled with ice and top with ginger beer. Garnish each drink with a mint sprig, lemon and orange wedges.

NOTE: This drink was inspired by Nick Van 'Tiki' Tiel.

blood orange frappé

SERVES 4

lemon sugar for rim (see page 242)
180 ml (6 fl oz) white rum
    (Havana Blanco works well)
60 ml (2 fl oz/¼ cup) Aperol
120 ml (4 fl oz) blood orange juice
20 ml (½ fl oz) lemon juice
20 ml (½ fl oz) sugar syrup (see page 238)

Half-rim four coupette glasses with the lemon sugar. Add the remaining ingredients to a blender, then add 4 scoops of crushed ice, blend and pour into the glasses.

the pink panther

SERVES 4

Pre-stain four champagne coupettes by twisting the orange zest to release the essence from the skin into the glass, then discard. Coat the sugar cubes with peach bitters. Drop a sugar cube into each glass and divide the gin, Lillet Blanc and crème de pêche equally between each glass. Top with the sparkling wine.

4 strips of orange zest
4 white sugar cubes
dash peach bitters per drink
180 ml (6 fl oz) gin
40 ml (1¼ fl oz) Lillet Blanc
60 ml (2 fl oz/¼ cup) crème de pêche
   (peach liqueur)
sparkling white wine

calvino

SERVES 4

Muddle (press down with a muddler or end of a rolling pin to crush) the grapes in four Boston glasses. Place the remaining ingredients in a shaker over ice and shake. Double strain into the glasses filled with cubed ice and top with crushed ice and skewered green grapes to garnish.

NOTE: This drink was inspired by Luke Reddington.

24 green grapes
160 ml (5¼ fl oz) apple brandy
60 ml (2 fl oz/¼ cup) Amaro Montenegro
40 ml (1¼ fl oz) coconut syrup
120 ml (4 fl oz/½ cup) grapefruit juice
skewered green grapes, to garnish

jamaican breakfast juice

SERVES 4

240 ml (8 fl oz) Jamaican golden rum
(Appleton's V/X works well)
240 ml (8 fl oz) orange juice
40 ml (1¼ fl oz) Pama liqueur
60 ml (2 fl oz/¼ cup) lime juice
60 ml (2 fl oz/¼ cup) sugar syrup
(see page 238)
4 teaspoons orange marmalade
3 dashes orange bitters
(Regan's works well)

Place all the ingredients in a shaker filled with ice. Shake and strain into four highball glasses filled with ice. Garnish each drink with an orange wedge, freshly grated nutmeg, a sprig of mint and an umbrella.

passionfruit swizzle

SERVES 4

180 ml (6 fl oz) golden rum
(Pampero works well)
40 ml (1¼ fl oz) lemon juice
60 ml (2 fl oz/¼ cup) crème de pêche
(peach liqueur)
20 ml (½ fl oz) sugar syrup (see page 238)
120 ml (4 fl oz) passionfruit pulp
4 passionfruit halves, to garnish

Place all the ingredients in a shaker filled with crushed ice, then swizzle (stir). Pour into four highball glasses, top with extra crushed ice and garnish each drink with the pulp of half a passionfruit.

pina colada

SERVES 4

Put all the ingredients in a blender and add 4 scoops of crushed ice, then blend until smooth. Strain into four chilled martini glasses and garnish with the pineapple crisps.

180 ml (6 fl oz) white rum (Havana Blanco works well)
60 ml (2 fl oz/¼ cup) pineapple juice
60 ml (2 fl oz/¼ cup) coconut milk
60 ml (2 fl oz/¼ cup) cream
20 ml (½ fl oz) sugar syrup (see page 238)
4 pineapple crisps, to garnish (see page 241)

mai tai

SERVES 4

Put all the ingredients in a Boston shaker filled with ice, shake and then strain into four old-fashioned glasses, filled with crushed ice. Garnish with mint sprigs and pineapple wedges.

180 ml (6 fl oz) white rum (Havana Blanco works well)
60 ml (2 fl oz/¼ cup) aged rum
60 ml (2 fl oz/¼ cup) orgeat syrup
80 ml (2½ fl oz/⅓ cup) lime juice
20 ml (½ fl oz) sugar syrup (see page 238)
4 Vietnamese mint sprigs and 4 fresh pineapple wedges, to garnish

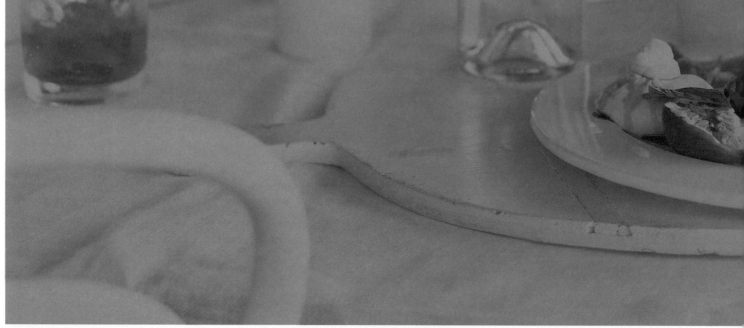

club med

The Mediterranean encompasses so many diverse flavours, from Italy right through to Turkey. I could write a book on these alone. The greatest thing about the region is that seasonal produce is truly the star – think ancient rows of olive trees, the freshest seafood, figs and buffalo mozzarella, does it get any better?

A few years ago, I was travelling through Victoria's high country and stopped at one of the local cafés and was lucky enough to order the right thing off the menu … don't you hate it when you order the wrong thing and your mate or the next table gets the meal you wish you had ordered? Well, this time everything I ordered at Coldstream Brewery, from head chef Scott Arthur, was unreal. This is one of the dishes I tried — great food, mate!

pumpkin, sage and parmesan fritters

MAKES 20

125 g (4½ oz) desiree potatoes
75 g (2½ oz) onion, thinly sliced
200 g (7 oz) raw grated pumpkin
3½ tablespoons finely chopped sage
35 g (1¼ oz) grated Grana Padano
1 free-range egg, lightly beaten
1 teaspoon sea salt
70 g (2½ oz) cornflour (cornstarch)
1 teaspoon vegetable oil
cottonseed oil, for frying
1 small handful sage leaves

caramelised onion crème fraîche
2 large brown onions, finely sliced
2 teaspoons balsamic vinegar
200 g (7 oz) crème fraîche
50 ml (1½ fl oz) double cream

To make the caramelised onion crème fraîche, sauté the onion in a frying pan over low-medium heat in a touch of oil until soft and caramelised. Add the balsamic vinegar then remove from the heat and cool completely. Combine with the crème fraîche and double cream and season with salt.

Cook the whole potato in a saucepan of cold salted water, simmer until just tender and then allow to cool slightly. Peel the potato while still warm and then coarsely grate.

Sweat the onion with a pinch of salt and a touch of oil in a pan over low heat until soft and translucent. Place in a bowl with the potato, pumpkin, chopped sage, Grana Padano, egg, sea salt, cornflour and vegetable oil and mix until combined. Refrigerate for 1 hour.

Heat some cottonseed oil in a wok or deep saucepan to 150°C (300°F). Deep-fry the sage leaves in batches until crisp. Drain on kitchen paper. Cook the fritters in batches, spooning tablespoons of the mixture into the oil and cooking for 5–6 minutes until golden brown and crisp. Drain on kitchen paper and serve with the crisp sage and caramelised onion crème fraîche.

Nothing says 'party' more than a platter of skewers (well for me anyway). I think anything put onto a skewer and grilled and presented with a lovely sauce or dressing is too good to refuse. This is a great little dish that I have eaten many times at my mate Maurice Terzini's restaurant, North Bondi Italian Food — a real winner and always delicious.

lamb skewers

MAKES 20

Soak 20 small bamboo skewers in water for 1 hour.

Place the diced lamb in a mixing bowl with the fresh oregano, dried oregano, garlic and olive oil. Mix thoroughly, cover with plastic wrap and marinate in the refrigerator for 2 hours.

Remove the skewers from the water. Remove the garlic and thread the lamb onto the skewers (about 3 pieces per skewer).

Drizzle the lamb skewers with a little olive oil. Preheat chargrill pan to high and cook the lamb skewers for 2 minutes, turn and cook the other side for 2 minutes or until cooked to your liking. Remove from the chargrill pan and drizzle with balsamic vinegar. Serve with lemon wedges and the extra oregano and oregano leaves.

600 g (1 lb 5 oz) boned lamb leg, diced into 2 cm (¾ inch) cubes
1 large handful of oregano leaves, plus extra to serve
2 tablepoons dried oregano
6 garlic cloves, roughly chopped
80 ml (2½ fl oz/⅓ cup) extra virgin olive oil
balsamic vinegar, for drizzling
lemon wedges, to serve

The most simple and utterly delicious offering in this book has to be the following recipe – ripe figs bursting with colour, burrata which is a fresh cheese made with mozzarella and cream, basil leaves and my favourite pantry ingredient, apple balsamic, all served on a crisp oven-baked piece of sourdough. The only thing that can top this is a piece of jamón Ibérico draped over the fig ... yum!

fig, basil and burrata

MAKES 20

1 day-old sourdough baguette
olive oil
5 ripe figs
2 balls burrata (buffalo mozzarella can be used instead)
1 handful of basil
lemon-infused extra virgin olive oil (or extra virgin olive oil is fine)
8 slices Jamón Ibérico (see note)
apple balsamic vinegar (see note)

Preheat the oven to 160°C (315°F/Gas 2–3). Slice the baguette into 5 mm (¼ inch) thick rounds and lay on a baking tray. Drizzle with olive oil and cook for 5 minutes or until just golden brown.

Slice the figs into quarters (or halved if they are small). Gently tear the burrata and lay on the croutons with the fig and some basil. Drizzle with the lemon-infused olive oil, tear the Jamón Ibérico and place on top, then drizzle with apple balsamic. Season with sea salt and cracked black pepper. Sprinkle with remaining basil to serve.

NOTE: Jamón Ibérico is the cured leg of black Iberian pig, fattened on grain and then foraged on acorns, available from Spanish delicatessens. You can buy apple balsamic from any good deli.

Perhaps one of the most unappealing canapés to look at is the
mushroom tart but as far as flavour and taste-bud satisfaction go,
these are the best you can get. When I'm catering I have a love/
hate relationship with them — I love to plate up beautiful, elegant
morsels but always shudder when I put these on the menu.
The reason I always include them is because I receive so many
compliments about them — so why don't you give them a go and
if you come up with a better way to present them, please let
me know!

wild mushroom tarts with sea salt

MAKES 20

Preheat the oven to 180°C (350°F/Gas 4).

Lay out the mushroom on a baking tray and drizzle with the oil. Bake in oven for 20 minutes or until golden. Place in a food processor and process until smooth, add the sea salt, pepper, porcini powder, dijon mustard, crème fraîche and egg yolks and process to combine.

To make the pastry cases, lay out the puff pastry sheets and prick with a fork. Cut out 20 circles with a 5.5 cm (2¼ inch) round cutter, then line greased mini muffin tin holes with the pastry.

Spoon or pipe the mix into the pastry and cook for 15 minutes or until the pastry is golden brown.

Remove the tarts from the tin, drizzle over the truffle oil and sprinkle with some extra sea salt.

600 g (1 lb 5 oz) field mushrooms, sliced
2 tablespoons olive oil
1 teaspoon sea salt
1 teaspoon cracked black pepper
2 teaspoons porcini powder
1 teaspoon dijon mustard
1 tablespoon crème fraîche
3 free-range egg yolks
2 sheets of frozen puff pastry, thawed
truffle oil, for drizzling

If you have my second book *My Table*, you might remember a recipe called Robbo's ribs — well, his other half, Sujeewa Roberts, cooked this for me at a recent shindig at their pad on the Northern beaches of Sydney. To say that I liked it is an understatement, I think I had 20 of them. They are delicious and here is the recipe.

haloumi and mint parcels

MAKES 20

10 sheets of filo pastry, cut in half
  (see note)
100 g (3½ oz) butter, melted
200 g (7 oz) haloumi cheese, sliced
  into 20 even pieces
1 large handful of mint
6 large cherry tomatoes, sliced into
  20 slices in total
125 ml (4 fl oz/½ cup) olive oil
lemon wedges, to serve
1 red chilli, sliced, to serve

caramelised onion
1 onion, sliced
olive oil
1 tablespoon caster (superfine) sugar
3 teaspoons balsamic vinegar

To make the caramelised onion, place the onion and a little oil in a saucepan over medium heat until the onion is soft, then add the sugar and balsamic vinegar and cook for 10 minutes or until caramelised. Remove from the heat and allow to cool.

Take half a sheet of filo pastry and brush with butter. Place 1 slice of haloumi, 1 mint leaf, 1 slice of cherry tomato, and a couple of strands of caramelised onion in the middle of one edge of the filo, season with salt and pepper. Fold the filo over the filling until you get a lovely bite-sized parcel. Repeat with the remaining ingredients.

Heat the olive oil in a non-stick frying pan over medium heat. Cook the parcels in batches until golden brown and the haloumi is nice and soft. Serve with lemon wedges and chilli.

NOTE: Buy fresh filo out of the fridge, rather than the freezer.

I love when salads are served at a party — they freshen and lighten things up which works a treat, especially when there is a lot of heavy food being served. This is an awesome salad that has loads of flavour but still feels lovely and light. It is also extremely easy to prepare beforehand. Just assemble and add toasted Lebanese bread and the dressing at the last minute.

fatoush salad with a yoghurt and tahini dressing

MAKES 20 SMALL GLASSES

2 large Lebanese breads

olive oil spray

1 teaspoon sumac

1 green or red capsicum (pepper), diced

3 vine-ripened tomatoes, diced

1 Lebanese (short) cucumber, seeded
    and chopped

½ red onion, thinly sliced

400 g (14 oz) tin cannellini or butter (lima)
    beans, rinsed and drained

20 white anchovies

1 handful of parsley leaves

1 small handful of coriander (cilantro)
    leaves

¼ cup coarsely chopped mint leaves

10 leaves baby cos (romaine) lettuce,
    roughly chopped

yoghurt and tahini dressing

1 garlic clove

2 tablespoons lemon juice

50 ml (1½ fl oz) extra virgin olive oil

250 g (9 oz/1 cup) plain yoghurt

3 tablespoons tahini

Preheat the oven to 160°C (315°F/Gas 2–3). Separate each piece of bread horizontally into 2 halves. Tear into 3–4 cm (1¼–1½ inch) pieces. Spread in a single layer on an oven tray and lightly spray with olive oil and dust with sumac. Bake for 5 minutes or until golden brown and crisp.

To make the yoghurt and tahini dressing, bruise the garlic clove with the side of a heavy knife. Place in a medium bowl with the remaining ingredients and stir well to combine. Season with sea salt and cracked black pepper.

In a large bowl, combine the capsicum, tomato, cucumber, onion, cannellini beans, white anchovies, parsley, coriander, mint and lettuce.

Place pieces of the toasted bread in small glasses with the salad. Remove the garlic clove from the dressing and spoon over the salad.

Now I know this recipe won't appeal to everyone but that's okay, the only reason a recipe appears in one of my books is that I love to both cook and eat it — full stop! It took me a while to appreciate offal but this is one of my favourite offal dishes to eat — it is simple to prepare and I think extremely rewarding. If you are not that fond of lamb's brains then simply substitute for lamb cutlets.

crumbed lamb's brains with salsa verde

MAKES 20

Carefully rinse the brains in cold water — they are delicate, so be gentle. Soak in cold water for 1 hour (this will help to draw out the blood).

To make the salsa verde, soak the bread in half the olive oil for 5 minutes. Blend all the ingredients in a blender with the remaining oil and season with salt and pepper.

Drain the brains and place in a saucepan over medium–high heat. Cover with cold water. Add a generous amount of salt, the peppercorns, parsley stalks and lemon juice. Bring just to the boil then reduce the heat and simmer for 4 minutes. Allow them to cool down in the liquid completely before removing. Remove with a slotted spoon and drain on kitchen paper. Season with a little salt, allow to cool.

Cut the brains into bite-sized pieces (about 5–6 per brain), dust in the flour, then the egg, then the combined breadcrumbs, parmesan and chopped parsley. Pour enough olive oil in a medium to large frying pan to cover 1 cm (½ inch) deep. Place over medium heat and shallow-fry the brains in batches for 3 minutes on each side or until golden brown. Remove to a warm plate while you repeat with the remaining brains. Serve on skewers with the lemon wedges and the salsa verde.

4 lamb's brains (180 g (6½ oz each)
10 black peppercorns
a few parsley stalks
juice of ½ lemon
plain (all-purpose) flour, for dusting
1 free-range egg, beaten
25 g (1 oz/⅓ cup) Japanese panko breadcrumbs
35 g (1¼ oz/⅓ cup) grated parmesan
3 tablespoons chopped parsley
olive oil for shallow-frying
lemon wedges, to serve

salsa verde

1 slice of stale bread
250 ml (9 fl oz/1 cup) olive oil
100 g (3½ oz/2 cups) basil leaves
100 g (3½ oz/2 cups) flat-leaf (Italian) parsley leaves
4 anchovies
50 g (1¾ oz) capers
3 tablespoons finely chopped cornichons
1 tablespoon lemon juice
50 g (1¾ oz/⅓ cups) pine nuts, toasted

Chefs and cooks are always looking for new ways to present food. Once we have the basics down as to what flavours work and why, it then becomes a question of how to make it look more appealing to the eye. This is one such dish — it tastes amazing and looks great but the challenge was how best to serve as a canapé to create a dramatic visual effect. We decided to wrap the ingredients into the bashed-out beef, roll it like sushi then cut it into bite-sized pieces. I think the end result is actually more satisfying to look at than regular carpaccio on a plate.

beef carpaccio with celeriac remoulade and truffled pecorino

MAKES 20

1 sourdough baguette

3 x 60 g (2¼ oz) portions of beef tenderloin cut against the grain

1 lemon, halved

1 tablespoon extra virgin olive oil

70 g (2½ oz) wild rocket (arugula), washed and picked

80 g (2¾ oz) finely grated truffled pecorino

extra truffled pecorino, shaved, for garnish

celeriac remoulade

½ celeriac

2 teaspoons wholegrain mustard

2 tablespoons chopped flat-leaf (Italian) parsley

4 tablespoons whole-egg mayonnaise

1 teaspoon truffle oil

Preheat the oven to 160°C (315°F/Gas 2–3). Slice the baguette into 5 mm (¼ inch) thick rounds and lay on a baking tray. Drizzle with olive oil, season with sea salt and cook for 5 minutes or until just golden brown.

To make the celeriac remoulade, peel and cut the celeriac into thin matchstick-sized strips. Mix in the mustard, parsley, mayonnaise, truffle oil and some salt and pepper.

Place the pieces of beef between sheets of plastic wrap and bash with a meat mallet until they are 2 mm (⅟₁₆ inch) thick. Remove the top layer of plastic wrap and squeeze over a few drops of lemon juice, a little olive oil and season with salt and cracked black pepper. Gently rub in with your fingertips. Place the celeriac remoulade along the centre of each piece of beef forming straight lines and leaving 3 cm (1¼ inches) at each end.

Dress the rocket with the remaining olive oil and some lemon juice and place on top of the celeriac. Scatter the grated truffled pecorino on top. Roll one side of the beef over the filling and roll tightly into a cigar shape. Cut the carpaccio into 2 cm (¾ inch) portions and place on the croutons. Serve with a little cracked black pepper and the extra shaved truffled pecorino.

NOTE: You can buy truffled pecorino at delicatessens or gourmet food stores.

Travelling through Spain a few times I have learned the subtle art of picking the good tapas bars from the bad ones. Usually a good measure of the place are the croquettes. A croquette is basically a fried roll with the main ingredient being either potato or a béchamel base filled with a variety of ingredients including salted cod, chicken, leek, cheese, jamón etc. I've eaten my fair share of croquettes and usually one in a tapas bar is enough. I believe they are a perfect party food that taste great.

spanish croquettes

MAKES 20

Heat the olive oil in a small saucepan over medium heat. Add the flour and cook for 3 minutes, stirring constantly. Gradually add the milk and the chicken stock, stirring continuously. Add the nutmeg, salt and cracked black pepper to taste. Cook over medium heat, stirring constantly, until the sauce is thickened and smooth.

Add the jamón and continue to cook for about 2–3 minutes over low heat, continuing to stir. Remove from the heat. Taste and adjust seasoning if necessary, add the cheese and stir through the mixture. Allow to cool for 10 minutes and refrigerate for at least 3 hours or until the mixture is cold. You could prepare the mixture the day before.

Place the breadcrumbs in a small wide bowl. Place the eggs in a separate small wide bowl and lightly beat with 2 teaspoons of water. Pour enough olive oil in a medium frying pan to cover 1 cm (½ inch) deep. Heat over medium heat. Cover your hands in flour, shape 1½ tablespoons of the mixture into oval-shaped croquettes. Dip the croquettes in the egg and coat with the breadcrumbs by rolling in the bowl. Fry the croquettes in batches for 4–5 minutes, turning several times, until golden. Remove the croquettes with a slotted spoon and drain on kitchen paper to absorb the excess oil. Serve immediately.

125 ml (4 fl oz/½ cup) olive oil
80 g (2¾ oz) plain (all-purpose) flour
375 ml (13 fl oz/1½ cups) milk
125 ml (4 fl oz/½ cup) chicken stock
½ teaspoon freshly grated nutmeg
90 g (3¼ oz/½ cup) very finely
    hand-minced jamón (or ham)
35 g (1¼ oz/¼ cup) grated
    Manchego cheese
Japanese panko breadcrumbs, for coating
2 free-range eggs
olive oil, for shallow-frying

emperor's elixir

Place all the ingredients in a shaker over ice and shake vigorously to emulsify the egg white. Strain into four tasting glasses filled with ice. Garnish with saffron threads.

180 ml (6 fl oz) golden rum (Havana 7YO
  works well)
60 ml (2 fl oz) saffron and honey syrup
  (see page 239)
120 ml (4 fl oz) blood orange juice
40 ml (1¼ fl oz) lemon juice
large dash of egg white
saffron threads, to garnish

verte

Place all ingredients in a shaker over ice and shake vigorously to emulsify the egg white. Double strain into four brandy balloons half-filled with ice and garnish with an apple fan and a sprig of rosemary.

120 ml (4 fl oz) Green Chartreuse
60 ml (2 fl oz) Pomme Verte (clear green
  apple liqueur)
120 ml (4 fl oz) cloudy apple juice
20 ml (½ fl oz) lime juice
2 rosemary sprigs
large dash of egg white
15 ml (½ fl oz) sugar syrup (see page 238)
4 apple fans with rosemary sprigs to scent,
  to garnish

campari cooler

SERVES 4

180 ml (6 fl oz) Campari
60 ml (2 fl oz) crème de peche
   (peach liqueur)
60 ml (2 fl oz) lemon juice
240 ml (8 fl oz) ruby red grapefruit juice
60 ml (2 fl oz) blood orange juice
18 mint leaves
4 pink grapefruit wedges and 4 mint
   sprigs, to garnish

Place all the ingredients in a jug over ice and stir. Serve in four long glasses filled with ice. Garnish each drink with a ruby red grapefruit wedge and mint sprig.

aperol sour

SERVES 4

120 ml (4 fl oz) Aperol
60 ml (2 fl oz) Cointreau
120 ml (4 fl oz) lemon juice
8 dashes of orange bitters
   (Regan's works well)
large dash of egg white
10 ml (2 teaspoons) sugar syrup
   (see page 238)
4 orange wedges, to garnish

Place all the ingredients in a shaker over ice and shake vigorously to emulsify the egg white. Strain into four glasses filled with ice and garnish each drink with an orange wedge.

st tropez spritzer

SERVES 4

240 ml (8 fl oz) pinot gris
60 ml (2 fl oz) Lillet Blanc
60 ml (2 fl oz) crème de peche
   (peach liqueur)
20 ml (½ fl oz) lemon juice
chilled sparkling mineral water, to serve
12 green grapes and 4 lemon twists,
   to garnish

Fill four glasses with ice. Mix together the pinot gris, Lillet Blanc, crème de peche and lemon juice and pour into the glasses. Top with the mineral water and garnish each drink with 3 grapes and a lemon twist.

mango sgropino

SERVES 4

180 ml (6 oz) mango sorbet
20 ml (½ fl oz) mango liqueur
20 ml (½ fl oz) lemon juice
240 ml (8 fl oz) Prosecco
4 mango crisps, to garnish
   (see page 241)

Place all the ingredients in a carafe and stir to combine. Strain into four champagne glasses and garnish each drink with a mango crisp.

limoncello and basil martini

SERVES 4

Place all the ingredients in a shaker over ice and shake vigorously to emulsify the egg white. Double strain into four chilled martini glasses and garnish each drink with a basil leaf.

NOTE: This recipe has been inspired by Naren Young and Marco Faraone.

180 ml (6 fl oz) gin (ideally you need
   a fresh, citrus-style gin for this, such
   as Plymouth)
60 ml (2 fl oz) limoncello
120 ml (4 fl oz) lemon juice
20 ml (½ fl oz) Cinzano Bianco
large dash of egg white
15 ml (½ fl oz) sugar syrup (see page 238)
6–8 basil leaves
4 basil leaves, extra, to garnish

garden blossom collins

SERVES 4

Place all the ingredients (except the Prosecco) in a jug and stir to combine. Pour into four highball glasses filled with ice. Top with Prosecco and garnish with an orange slice.

180 ml (6 fl oz) gin (ideally you need
   a fresh, citrus-style gin for this,
   such as Plymouth)
3 ml (½ teaspoon) orange blossom water
60 ml (2 fl oz) lemon juice
60 ml (2 fl oz) Cointreau
20 ml (½ fl oz) sugar syrup (see page 238)
Prosecco
4 orange slices, to garnish

spice nights

Asian cuisine is special and linked intrinsically to culture and lifestyle. Bites bursting with sour, salt, spice and lime lend themselves perfectly to canapés – it's all about balance and seasoning.

I love visiting a new restaurant and seeing something I haven't seen before. A little while ago I happened to visit Coda bar and restaurant in the heart of Melbourne's CBD. The chef/owner Adam D'Sylva has created a menu that is unique, with each dish calling out to be eaten. Luckily the menu is made up of lots of bite-sized morsels as I ingested pretty much the entire range in one sitting. This dish, however, was a real standout – wonderfully crisp betel leaves filled with moist prawn mousse and fried to perfection.

crispy prawn and tapioca betel leaf

MAKES 20

6 garlic cloves, chopped
1 green banana chilli, chopped
1 x 4 cm (1½ inch) piece of
    ginger, chopped
300 g (10½ oz) raw prawn (shrimp) meat
30 ml (1 fl oz) oyster sauce
30 ml (1 fl oz) fish sauce
3 teaspoons caster (superfine) sugar
12 kaffir lime leaves, finely sliced
¾ cup coriander (cilantro) leaves
vegetable oil, for deep-frying
20 large betel leaves
tapioca flour, for dusting

tapioca batter
100 g (3½ oz/⅔ cup) tapioca flour
100 g (3½ oz/⅔ cup) rice flour
ice-cold soda water

soy vinegar dipping sauce
250 ml (9 fl oz/1 cup) light soy sauce
150 ml (5 fl oz) rice vinegar

Using a mortar and pestle, pound the garlic, chilli and ginger to a smooth paste. Place the paste, prawn meat, oyster sauce, fish sauce, sugar, kaffir lime leaves and coriander in a blender and blend until smooth.

Heat the oil to 180°C (350°F) in a wok or deep saucepan.

To make the tapioca batter, combine the flours in a bowl then gradually whisk in the soda water until it is a pouring consistency.

To make the dipping sauce combine the light soy and rice vinegar. Place the betel leaves shiny side down, spoon 1 tablespoon of the prawn mixture onto each leaf and close by bringing the tip and bottom of the leaf together. Dust in tapioca flour and shake off any excess. Then dip the leaf in the tapioca batter and drain off the excess. (The batter may start to thicken as it stands so you can add a little more soda water as necessary.)

Deep-fry in batches for 4 minutes until crispy and cooked through. Drain on kitchen paper, season with sea salt and serve with the soy vinegar dipping sauce.

My catering business does a lot of top-end catering around the country and this item always stands out as a clear winner. It has the most wonderful dressing and the crispy garlic is a nice surprise that will wow your guests. Tataki is a finely sliced, piece of seared meat that is rare inside – you can use kingfish, tuna, salmon or beef but to take it to the next level, use a lovely piece of wagyu.

wagyu tataki with crispy garlic and shallots

SERVES 20

To make the ponzu, place all the ingredients in a bowl and mix well.

To make the tataki dressing, combine all the ingredients a bowl.

Rinse the spring onions under water for a few minutes then drain and refrigerate.

Heat 2 cm (¾ inch) of vegetable oil in a small deep saucepan over medium heat. Sauté the garlic slices until golden then strain and drain on kitchen paper. Sprinkle with salt.

Preheat a chargrill pan to high, lightly brush the beef fillet with some olive oil and season with salt and pepper. Sear the beef on all sides until medium rare.

To assemble, slice the beef into thin slivers and arrange in small dishes or shot glasses. Pour half a teaspoon of the tataki dressing and half a teaspoon of the ponzu over each piece. Add a couple of garlic crisps to the wagyu and finish with the chives and spring onion.

2 spring onions (scallions),
  finely shredded
vegetable oil, for frying
3 garlic cloves, thinly sliced
250 g (9 oz) wagyu sirloin
olive oil
1 tablespoon finely snipped chives

ponzu
½ white onion, finely diced
1 garlic clove, finely chopped
1 tablespoon grapeseed oil
1 tablespoon lemon juice
1 tablespoon rice vinegar
1 tablespoon soy sauce
¼ teaspoon finely chopped ginger

tataki dressing
2½ tablespoons soy sauce
80 ml (2½ fl oz/⅓ cup) rice vinegar
1 teaspoon bonito flakes (optional)

This may be the most popular finger food in the world — created by the Chinese in the 1300s and perfected over the next 700 odd years — I'd say you're in trusted hands with this dish. It is always a crowd-pleaser and the best part is, it's so easy to make. You can buy everything you need in Chinatown or your local Asian grocer.

peking duck rolls – my way

MAKES 20

pancake

75 g (2½ oz/½ cup) plain
    (all-purpose) flour
2 tablespoons cornflour (cornstarch)
60 ml (2 fl oz/¼ cup) milk
2 eggs
40 g (1½ oz) butter, melted

1 Peking duck (from a Chinese
    barbecue shop)
200 ml (7 fl oz) hoisin sauce
50 ml (1½ fl oz) plum sauce
4 baby cos (romaine) lettuces,
    leaves separated and washed
6 spring onions (scallions), cut
    into batons
2 cucumbers, cut into batons
1½ tablespoons toasted sesame seeds

To make the pancakes, combine the flours in a bowl, make a well in the centre and whisk in the milk, eggs, half the butter and 80 ml (2½ fl oz/⅓ cup) water. Whisk until the batter is smooth. Pour into a jug. Cover and stand for 15 minutes.

Heat a small non-stick frying pan over low–medium heat. Brush with the remaining butter. Pour 2 tablespoons of batter into the frying pan and spread to form a thin pancake about 15 cm (6 inches) in diameter. Cook for 2 minutes. Turn and cook for a further minute. Transfer to a plate. Repeat with the remaining batter adding a little more milk if it gets too thick. Cool the pancakes and shred 2 of them to use as garnish. (You could use some of the remaining pancakes cut in half to serve the duck if you like.)

Remove the skin and meat from the duck. Thinly slice both the skin and meat. Combine the hoisin and plum sauces. Lay 20 lettuce leaves on platters and top with some shredded duck meat and skin, spring onion and cucumber. To serve, spoon over some of the sauce, sprinkle with the sesame seeds and top with the shredded pancake.

I absolutely love serving this dish. The main component here is, of course, the braised pork, which is delicious by itself or for something more substantial, serve it with steamed brown rice and Asian vegetables. For a canapé or finger food option, why not try making these simple steamed buns as something fun to serve the pork on. The addition of the pickled cucumber really cuts through the richness of the pork and a touch of hot chilli sauce, fresh Asian herbs and some toasted sesame seeds make this dish a real standout.

steamed pork buns

MAKES 18

To braise the pork, combine all the ingredients (except the pork) in a saucepan and bring to the boil. Add the pork cheek and allow it to boil again, then turn down to a simmer, cover the surface with baking paper and cook for 1–1½ hours or until tender. Allow the pork to cool in the stock, then remove and shred the meat. Strain the liquid, reserving some masterstock to moisten the pork when reheating to serve.

To make the buns, combine the yeast and 170 ml (5½ fl oz/⅔ cup) warm water in the bowl of an electric mixer fitted with a dough hook. Add the flour, sugar, milk powder, sea salt, baking powder, bicarbonate of soda and start the mixer on medium speed. Add the vegetable oil and mix until the dough comes together. Reduce speed to low and continue to mix for 8–10 minutes. Remove the dough, place in a greased bowl, cover with a tea towel (dish towel) and allow to rest in a warm place for about an hour or until the dough has doubled in size.

Bring the rice vinegar and sugar to the boil in a small saucepan. Allow to cool. An hour before serving, combine the sliced cucumber with the vinegar mixture and set aside.

Line bamboo steamer baskets with greased, non-stick baking paper. Knock the dough back and cut into 3 pieces. Roll each piece into a sausage shape and cut each into 6. Roll into balls on a lightly floured surface. Flatten with the palm of your hand and use a rolling pin to roll them into 6 cm (2½ inch) diameter discs. Steam in batches for 4–6 minutes or until cooked through.

Meanwhile, reheat the pork in a small saucepan over low heat with some of the reserved masterstock. Assemble the canapé by spreading a thin layer of chilli sauce on the top of the hot steamed bun, add the cucumber, top with the braised pork and finish with the coriander and chilli. Serve warm.

braised pork

325 ml (11 fl oz) Shaoxing
   rice wine
150 ml (5 fl oz) soy sauce
200 g (7 oz) caster (superfine) sugar
1 knob ginger, sliced
5 garlic cloves, bruised
3 spring onions (scallions),
   roughly chopped
3 star anise
400 g (14 oz) pork cheek (or you could
   use pork neck)

100 ml (3½ fl oz) rice vinegar
100 g (3½ oz) sugar
2 Lebanese (short) cucumbers, finely
   sliced into rounds
2 tablespoons hot chilli sauce
coriander (cilantro) leaves, to serve
4 long red chillies, seeded and
   finely sliced

pork bun base

3 teaspoons active dry yeast
300 g (10½ oz/2¼ cups) strong flour
55 g (2 oz/¼ cup) sugar
1½ tablespoons instant skim milk powder
2 teaspoons sea salt
¼ teaspoon baking powder
¼ teaspoon bicarbonate of soda
   (baking soda)
35 ml (1 fl oz) vegetable oil

I'm not sure where this canapé came from – I've had so many great chefs work with me over the past 20 years and they all bring with them ideas from their previous jobs. The joy is to incorporate that knowledge into your own business to make it constantly evolving and stimulating – this dish has been a favourite on our canapé menus for the last decade and while it's a wonderful vegetarian option, it will also have meat lovers hovering around the platter.

spiced eggplant and tofu cabbage rolls with chilli jam

MAKES 20 PIECES

To make the chilli jam, heat the oil in a frying pan and sauté the onion and capsicum until soft. Add the remaining ingredients and simmer for 30 minutes. Blend until smooth and then season.

Heat some vegetable oil in a frying pan and fry the eggplant in batches until golden, drain on kitchen paper.

In a wok or large frying pan, add the peanut oil, garlic, ginger, chilli and bulb spring onion and cook over medium heat until just starting to colour. Add the mushroom, eggplant, soy sauce, black vinegar, Shaoxing rice wine, fish sauce, white pepper and sugar. Simmer for 5 minutes then take off the heat and add the tofu and coriander. Set aside to cool.

Wash the cabbage leaves in plenty of water. Blanch in boiling water (beware not to overcook – no more than 40 seconds per leaf) and refresh in iced water. The leaves should be translucent and firm. Drain on a tea towel (dish towel), allow to cool and trim off some of the thicker bottom end of the leaf.

Take one cabbage leaf and place one tablespoon of filling in the centre. Fold both sides inwards and roll over into a tight parcel. Serve at room temperature with a touch of chilli jam on top.

NOTE: In the chilli jam, use hot chilli paste if you like it spicy. If you prefer less heat go for a mild chilli paste.

vegetable oil, for frying
2 large eggplants (aubergines), peeled and
    cut into 2 cm (¾ inch) dice
1 tablespoon peanut oil
1 teaspoon finely chopped garlic
1 teaspoon finely chopped ginger
3 red chillies, finely chopped
4 bulb spring onions (scallions), diced
4 black cloud ear fungus
    (or shiitake mushrooms), finely sliced
1 tablespoon soy sauce
1 tablespoon Chinese black vinegar
2 tablespoons Shaoxing rice wine
2 teaspoons fish sauce
½ teaspoon white pepper
2 teaspoons sugar
150 g (5½ oz) silken tofu, finely chopped
1 large handful of coriander
    (cilantro) leaves
1 Chinese cabbage (wong bok),
    leaves separated

chilli jam
1 tablespoon olive oil
1 red onion, diced
1 red capsicum (pepper), chopped
1 punnet of cherry tomatoes
10 banana chillies, seeded and chopped
2 tablespoons chopped coriander (cilantro)
    roots and stems
95 g (3¼ oz/½ cup) soft brown sugar
2 tablespoons chilli paste (see note)
1-2 tablespoons fish sauce
1 lemon, peeled and chopped, pips removed

Travelling through Vietnam you get to experience a wide variety of mind-blowing dishes but on most menus — there will be a fresh spring roll of some description. I tried these at nearly every restaurant or street stall that I visited and though they varied from place to place, one thing was sure, they were always great for a snack to enliven the palate. Give these a go — they are a lot of fun to make and the best part is they are both healthy and tasty.

fresh prawn spring rolls with nuoc cham

MAKES 20

170 ml (5½ fl oz/⅔ cup) rice vinegar
165 g (5¾ oz/¾ cup) sugar
1 bird's eye chilli, cut in half lengthways
250 g (9 oz/1⅔ cups) grated carrot
250 g (9 oz/1¾ cups) finely shredded daikon
1 small cos (romaine) lettuce
20 x 20 cm (8 x 8 inch) diameter round rice paper wrappers
1 large handful of coriander (cilantro) leaves
1 large handful of Vietnamese mint leaves
20 cooked king prawns (shrimp), peeled and deveined, tail left intact

nuoc cham

5 tablespoons sugar
80 ml (2½ fl oz/⅓ cup) fish sauce
125 ml (4 fl oz/½ cup) lime or lemon juice
1 garlic clove, crushed
1 or more bird's eye chillies, seeded and sliced

To make the nuoc cham, whisk together the sugar, 3 tablespoons of water, fish sauce and lime juice in a bowl until the sugar is completely dissolved. Add the garlic and chilli and allow to stand for 30 minutes before serving.

Bring the rice vinegar and sugar to the boil with the chilli. Stir to dissolve the sugar and make a pickling liquid. Set aside and cool down completely. In a bowl, combine the carrot and daikon with the pickling liquid and let it sit for at least an hour before serving, stirring occasionally. Strain, set the vegetables aside and discard the liquid and chilli halves.

Finely shred the lettuce.

To make a spring roll, briefly dip a rice paper wrapper in a bowl of warm water until soft and translucent. Lay on a clean work surface and place a small amount of lettuce on to the wrapper, closer to one edge, and top with the pickled carrot, daikon and herbs.

Make a few small cuts with a sharp knife to the underside of each prawn (this will help to straighten the prawn a little). Place the prawn on top of the other ingredients with the tail on the outside edge of the wrapper. Fold to enclose. Repeat with the remaining ingredients.

Yuzu is a citrus fruit from Asia with a unique flavour that is perfectly matched to seafood. This is a classic Japanese dressing that works with just about any type of seafood you choose to chop, slice and serve raw. Some of my favourites are scampi, prawns (shrimp), scallops, any type of white-fleshed fish and also the fattier fish such as salmon, trout, mackerel and tuna. You could even just drizzle it over a freshly shucked oyster for a match made in heaven.

snapper tartare with yuzu dressing

MAKES 20

Dice the snapper into small 1 cm (½ inch) cubes and place in a chilled bowl.

To make the dressing combine the yuzu juice, soy sauce, pepper, garlic and grapeseed oil in a jar and shake well.

Pour over the snapper and toss to coat.

Divide between small glasses or spoons and serve immediately with the jalapeño and shiso to garnish.

NOTE: Yuzu juice has a distinctive sharp taste and is available bottled from Japanese supermarkets. You could substitute with fresh lemon juice if you like.

250 g (9 oz) snapper fillet, skin off
50 ml (1½ fl oz) yuzu juice
1¼ tablespoons soy sauce
½ teaspoon freshly cracked pepper
½ teaspoon finely grated garlic
6 tablespoons grapeseed oil
1 jalapeño chilli, finely diced, to serve
small shiso leaves or chopped coriander
(cilantro) leaves, to serve

I was recently in LA cooking with Curtis Stone and the legendary Wolfgang Pucks catering team for 'G'Day USA'. We had to cater for 800 people. The following recipe is one of the canapés I created for the night. When I serve this at a function, I normally present the fish salad on betel leaves (edible leaves from South-East Asia that have medicinal qualities). However, on arrival in LA, I found that betel leaves weren't available, so I decided to serve the fish on crispy fried won tons as an alternative. To be honest, I think the won tons worked better as they are easier to handle and add great texture to the end result. For a larger serving, just add some finely sliced green mango, papaya or glass noodles for a refreshing salad.

smoked fish salad on crispy won tons

MAKES 20

canola oil, for deep-frying

20 won ton wrappers

1 smoked rainbow trout (approximately 200 g (7 oz) flesh)

2 long red chillies, seeded and finely shredded

1 large handful of mint leaves, torn

3 kaffir lime leaves, finely sliced

1 large handful of coriander (cilantro) leaves

125 g (4½ oz/½ cup) good-quality chilli jam (see page 76)

4 tablespoons crispy shallots (see page 154)

50 g (1¾ oz) salmon or trout roe

nam jim

4 red Asian shallots, chopped

2 red bird's eye chillies

2 garlic cloves

1 teaspoon chopped coriander (cilantro) root

100 ml (3½ fl oz) lime juice

75 g (2¾ oz) grated palm sugar (jaggery)

50 ml (1½ fl oz) fish sauce

To make the nam jim dressing, pound the shallots, chillies, garlic and coriander root using a mortar and pestle and then add the lime juice. Season with the palm sugar and fish sauce for a balance of hot, sour, salty and sweet.

Heat the canola oil to 180°C (350°F) in a wok or deep saucepan. Separate the won tons and gently fry in batches for 1–2 minutes turning once until light golden. Drain on kitchen paper and allow to cool.

Flake the smoked trout and combine with the chilli, mint, kaffir lime leaves and coriander leaves. Dress with some·of the nam jim. Place a teaspoon of chilli jam on top of the fried won ton wrappers, place a small mound of the fish salad on top and then sprinkle with the crispy shallots and top with the salmon roe.

One of the most loved foods from my childhood were the chicken wings my mum would make for me using an assortment of Asian sauces and spices from the pantry. I wanted to include a grown-up version in this book where your fingers don't get sticky but they could still bring back those memories of sucking the meat off the bone, so here it is. It is important that you marinate the chicken to really let the flavour penetrate into the flesh as we're serving the sauce separate and if your guests don't double dip then at least the chicken tastes delicious just by itself.

fried crispy chicken with black vinegar dressing

MAKES 20

Remove the wing tips from the chicken wings then cut each wing in half. Place the Shaoxing rice wine, garlic and star anise in a non-reactive dish. Add the chicken and marinate overnight. Steam the chicken pieces in batches, in a steamer basket set over a pot of simmering water, for 20 minutes or until cooked through and then allow to cool on kitchen paper.

To make the black vinegar sauce combine all the ingredients together.

Heat the oil to 180°C (350°F) in a wok or deep saucepan. Season the tapioca flour with salt and pepper. Lightly toss the chicken pieces in the tapioca flour and shake off any excess. Deep-fry the chicken wings in batches for about 5 minutes or until golden brown and cooked through. Drain on kitchen paper and sprinkle with sea salt.

Garnish the black vinegar sauce with the extra ginger and serve.

2 kg (4 lb 8 oz) chicken wings
250 ml (9 fl oz/1 cup) Shaoxing
 rice wine
3 garlic cloves, chopped
2 star anise
vegetable oil, for frying
tapioca flour, for dusting

black vinegar sauce
125 ml (4 fl oz/½ cup) Chinese
 black vinegar
2 tablespoons peanut oil
1 tablespoon grated ginger, plus extra
 finely shredded ginger to serve
1 teaspoon kecap manis (sweet
 soy sauce)
¼ cup chopped coriander (cilantro) leaves

vera

SERVES 1

50 ml (1½ fl oz) gin (Hendricks works well
  due to its floral notes)
10 ml (2 teaspoons) crème de pêche
  (peach liqueur)
30 ml (1 fl oz) sweetened aloe vera water
  (available at health food stores)
5 ml (1 teaspoon) lemon juice
dash of peach bitters
sparkling mineral water
1 Vietnamese mint sprig, to garnish

Place all the ingredients, except the mineral water, in a highball glass filled with ice. Stir thoroughly. Top with the mineral water and a mint sprig to garnish.

zen berry

SERVES 1

45 ml (1½ fl oz) white rum (Havana Blanco
  works well)
10 ml (2 teaspoons) crème de framboise
  (raspberry liqueur) or you can use your
  own raspberry syrup (see page 239)
5 ml (1 teaspoon) Joseph Cartron
  coconut liqueur
30 ml (1 fl oz) fresh young coconut juice
6 raspberries
5 ml (1 teaspoon) sugar syrup
  (see page 238)
3 raspberries on a skewer dusted in
  coconut sugar (see page 242), to garnish

Place all the ingredients in a shaker over ice and shake vigorously to break the raspberries in the shaker. Double strain the mixture into a chilled martini glass. Add the coconut-sugar-dusted raspberries to garnish.

asian iced tea

SERVES 4

Place the lime wedges, mint and sugar into a carafe or decanter and bruise. Add crushed ice and the remaining ingredients. Pour into four glasses filled with ice and garnish with the apple crisp.

NOTE: Make and strain the jasmine green tea and sweeten to taste while still warm.

12 lime wedges

24 mint leaves

4 teaspoons white sugar

180 ml (6 fl oz) blended whisky

300 ml (10½ fl oz) sweetened jasmine
    green tea, cooled to room temperature
    (see note)

100 ml (3½ fl oz) clear apple juice

4 apple crisps, to garnish
    (see page 241)

oriental spice

SERVES 1

Place all the ingredients in a shaker over ice. Shake vigorously to emulsify the egg white. Strain into an old fashioned glass over cubed ice and top with crushed ice. Sprinkle over the cinnamon and nutmeg and garnish with the candied chilli.

45 ml (1½ fl oz) single malt whisky
    (Glenfiddich 12YO works well)

15 ml (½ fl oz) Grand Marnier

15 ml (½ fl oz) lemon juice

30 ml (1 fl oz) mandarin juice

3 thin slices of chilli

dash of egg white

pinch of ground cinnamon and freshly
    grated nutmeg on surface with a
    candied chilli half (see page 241),
    to garnish

floral delight

SERVES 1

45 ml (1½ fl oz) vodka
15 ml (½ fl oz) Pomme Verte (clear,
    green apple liqueur)
30 ml (1 fl oz) pineapple juice
5 ml (1 teaspoon) lime juice
3 kaffir lime leaves
extra kaffir lime leaf, to garnish

Place all the ingredients in a shaker over ice and shake vigorously. Strain into a chilled martini glass and garnish with a floating kaffir lime leaf.

vietnamese crush

SERVES 1

1 lemon wedge
vanilla sugar (see page 242)
4 Vietnamese mint leaves
15 ml (½ fl oz) spiced apricot and
    vanilla syrup (see page 239)
45 ml (1½ fl oz) single malt whisky
    (floral notes in single malt whisky like
    Glemorangie work well)
15 ml (½ fl oz) Cointreau
30 ml (1 fl oz) lemon juice
sparkling mineral water
sliced dried apricots, to garnish

Use the lemon wedge to run around the rim of a highball glass, then dip half of the rim of the glass into the vanilla sugar. Tear the mint leaves and add to a shaker over ice with the remaining ingredients (except the mineral water). Shake and pour into the glass. Top with crushed ice, add the mineral water, stir, top with more crushed ice and garnish with the sliced dried apricots to finish.

lina's lychee martini

SERVES 1

Stain a martini glass with the lemon zest, then discard. Place all the ingredients in a shaker over ice. Shake and strain into the glass and drop a lychee in to garnish (you can make this 2 or 3 if you really love lychees).

zest of 1 lemon
50 ml (1½ fl oz) gin (for this drink a fresh citrus gin like Plymouth works well)
10 ml (2 teaspoons) lychee liqueur
30 ml (1 fl oz) lychee juice
5 ml (1 teaspoon) Lillet Blanc
3 dashes peach bitters
lychee, peeled, to garnish

bangkok punch

SERVES 1

Place all the ingredients in a shaker over ice. Shake the drink and then strain into an old fashioned glass filled with ice and garnish with the rambutans.

45 ml (1½ fl oz) single malt whisky (Glenfiddich 12YO works well)
15 ml (½ fl oz) crème de gingembre (ginger liqueur) or you can use your own ginger syrup (see page 239)
75 ml (2¼ fl oz) pineapple juice
5 ml (1 teaspoon) lime juice
5 ml (1 teaspoon) lemongrass syrup (see page 239)
2 rambutans, peeled
2 full rambutans with their skin on, to garnish

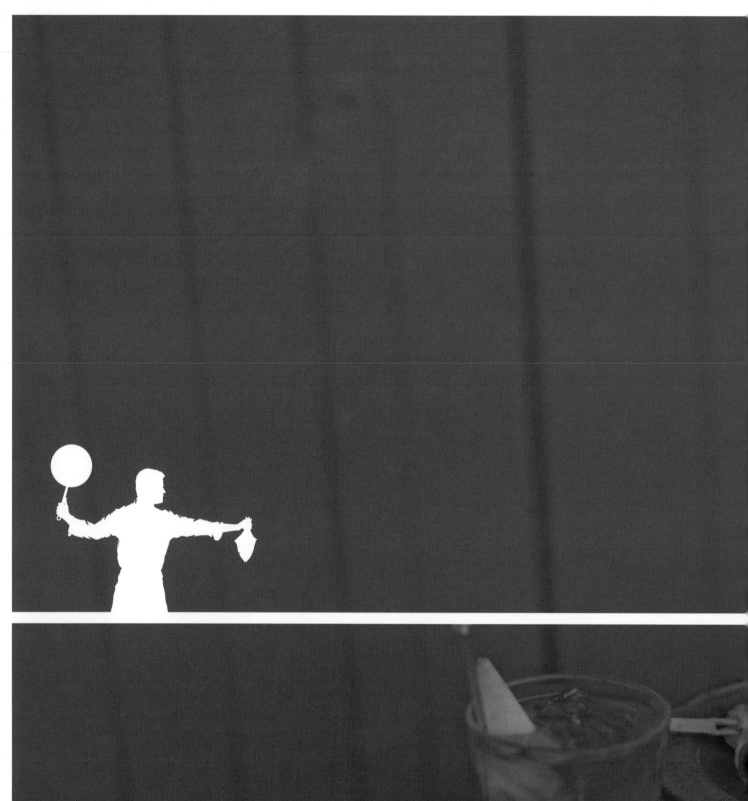

carnival

The use of spice and fresh produce works so well with entertaining — the flavours are deliciously addictive. This chapter features cocktails ranging from the heat of Mexico, using high-end 100% agave tequila, to drinks made with Mezcal for smoky South American nights. South of Mexico is a continent of diverse cultures and our chilli martini shows that, heart and soul.

This is an elaborate toasted sandwich – great for finger-food parties and vegetarians. Make sure when you serve it you have some freshly cut limes to squeeze over and sea salt to sprinkle on top.

goat's cheese, caramelised onion and fire-roasted pepper quesadilla

MAKES 24

caramelised onion
4 red onions, peeled and finely diced
2½ tablespoons extra virgin olive oil
2 tablespoons soft brown sugar
100 ml (3½ fl oz) red wine vinegar

4 red capsicums (peppers)
8 soft flour tortillas
200 g (7 oz) soft chevre-style
   goat's cheese
1 large handful of basil leaves
lime wedges, to serve

To make the caramelised onion, gently cook the onions with the oil, sugar and vinegar in a heavy-based pan for 20 minutes until it becomes translucent and caramelised. Set aside to cool.

Preheat a barbecue or grill (broiler) to high heat. Rub the capsicums with a little oil and cook on the barbecue. Cook on all sides, turning until the outer skin is charred and black. When cool, scrape away the black outer skin, cut them in half, remove any seeds, then finely dice the flesh.

Lay out 4 of the tortillas and spread evenly with the goat's cheese. Scatter the caramelised onion, capsicum and basil leaves evenly over the goat's cheese. Place the rest of the tortillas on top forming a sandwich.

Preheat a barbecue hot plate or frying pan over medium–high heat. Cook the tortillas for 2 minutes on each side until crisp and the cheese starts to melt. Remove from the barbecue and cut each into 6 wedges, serve hot.

NOTE: Don't be tempted to wash the charred skin of the capsicum as this will detract from the smoky flavour you are looking for.

If you have read my other books, you'll be well aware that I have a love affair with oysters. The best way to serve them is freshly shucked and straight down the hatch but in reality, we can't always get our hands on live oysters. We end up buying pre-shucked oysters and the problem with these is they don't retain all those lovely juices so we need to serve them with great accompaniments. This simple granita is a fun way to serve oysters at your next party.

freshly shucked oysters with mojito granita

MAKES 20

In a mixing jug, muddle (press down with a muddler or end of a rolling pin to crush) the lime wedges, mint leaves and sugar, then add the rum and top with 80 ml (2½ fl oz/⅓ cup) water and the lime juice.

Pour into a clean loaf tin, remove the lime wedges and freeze for 2 hours. As it starts to set, run a fork through the frozen mixture to rough it up into ice shavings.

Arrange the oysters on a platter and served topped with some granita.

8 lime wedges
24 mint leaves
2 tablespoons sugar
240 ml (8 fl oz) Havana Blanco rum
2 tablespoons lime juice
20 Sydney rock oysters, freshly shucked

Crab … tick. Mango … tick. Limes … tick. This recipe brings back memories of the tropics. Whenever I visit the top of Australia, the things that always stand out to me are the quality of the crabs, mangoes and limes — and generally the best dishes are created when all of the ingredients are locally sourced. This is a great use of tropical produce to create a fun snack at your next party.

corn chip crusted crab cakes with mango lime mojo

MAKES 20

mojo
2 mangoes, peeled and diced
110 g (3¾ oz/½ cup) grated palm sugar
juice of 5 limes
1 tablespoon finely grated ginger
1 pickled jalapeño chilli, chopped

1 large potato
½ sweet potato
2 teaspoons sour cream
1 large handful coriander
   (cilantro) leaves, chopped
250 g (9 oz) cooked crabmeat
pinch of cayenne pepper
1 egg
125 ml (4 fl oz/½ cup) milk
plain (all-purpose) flour, for dusting
200 g (7 oz) corn chips, crushed
   to make crumbs
vegetable oil, for deep-frying

To make the mojo, place the mangoes, palm sugar, lime juice and ginger in a saucepan and gently simmer for 30 minutes then remove from the heat. Cool slightly then blend until smooth, refrigerate to chill.

Peel and cut both the potatoes into even pieces then steam until tender. Crush the potato mix (not too much, they need a little texture), then add the sour cream, coriander and crabmeat, season with salt, pepper and cayenne. Cool in the refrigerator for at least 1 hour to set the mixture slightly. Whisk together the egg and milk. Roll 1½ tablespoons of the mixture into balls, roll in flour then egg wash and finally crushed corn chips.

Heat some vegetable oil in a wok or deep saucepan to 180°C (350°F). Cook the crab cakes in batches, frying for 2 minutes each side until golden and crisp. Drain on kitchen paper and serve with the mojo sprinkled with the jalapeño.

Scallops were designed to be the perfect party-food ingredient — they are just the right size and shape to pop in the mouth in one bite. More importantly though, they are the princess of the sea and very little has to be done to them to appreciate their flavour. This is a cool way to add a bit of Mexican spice to your next party — if you don't have tortillas to use as the base you can just use a baguette sliced thinly and toasted in the oven until golden.

scallop tostadas with smoked avocado and salsa fresco

MAKES 24

Preheat the oven to 160°C (315°F/Gas 2–3). Cut the tortillas into 4 cm (1½ inch) round shapes or similar-sized wedges and place on baking tray. Drizzle with a little olive oil and sea salt, bake in the oven for 8–10 minutes or until crisp and golden.

Preheat a barbecue grill to medium–high. Cut the avocados into halves, remove the stones and cook flesh-side down for 2–3 minutes, remove from the skin and blend with the sour cream in a food processor. Add the juice of 1 lime and season with salt, pepper and a dash of Tabasco sauce.

To make the salsa, core the tomatoes, cut them into quarters and deseed. Using a sharp knife, finely dice the flesh and mix with the onion, oil, coriander and the remaining lime juice. Season with salt and pepper. Increase the barbecue heat to high. Lightly sear the scallops on a lightly oiled hotplate. To construct, place a teaspoon of avocado mix on the tortilla then a scallop and finally the salsa.

3 flour tortillas
olive oil
2 avocados
80 g (2¾ oz) sour cream
juice of 4 limes
Tabasco sauce
24 sea scallops

salsa fresco
2 roma (plum) tomatoes
¼ red onion, finely chopped
80 ml (2½ fl oz/⅓ cup) extra virgin olive oil
1 handful of coriander (cilantro) leaves, finely chopped

This is a stunning dish to serve at your next party — it's a simple recipe that really packs a punch. The thing I love about it is the presentation on the witlof leaf, it not only looks great but it's a superb vegetable to eat and is a great vessel to serve in. If you can't find witlof, the next best thing for this recipe would be some little discs of deep-fried tortilla or just some shot glasses and an oyster fork.

kingfish ceviche with blood orange and smoked chilli oil

SERVES 20

In a heavy-based saucepan over medium–high heat reduce the blood orange juice to a syrupy consistency then add the lemon juice and cool. In a separate saucepan heat the extra virgin olive oil and chipotle chilli until hot then let cool, whisk together the syrup and the infused oil to form the dressing.

Cut the kingfish fillets into 2 cm (¾ inch) dice. In a mixing bowl, combine the fish, orange, macadamia nuts, onion and coriander and dress liberally with blood orange dressing. Season with sea salt and pepper then leave the mixture to marinate for 20 minutes.

Cut the witlof into individual leaves. Spoon the ceviche mixture on top, scatter with coriander leaves and serve.

NOTE: Valencia oranges can be substituted if blood oranges are not available. Chipotle chilli is a delicious smoked, dried jalapeño.

600 ml (21 fl oz) blood orange juice

100 ml (3½ fl oz) lemon juice

300 ml (10½ fl oz) extra virgin olive oil

½ chipotle chilli, finely chopped

400 g (14 oz) kingfish fillets, skin removed

4 blood oranges, peeled, segmented and diced

70 g (2½ oz/½ cup) chopped macadamia nuts

½ red onion, finely chopped

1 small handful of coriander (cilantro) leaves, chopped

3 heads of purple witlof (chicory)

coriander (cilantro) leaves, to serve

When thinking about your next party, good dishes to serve are raw seafood dishes like sushi, tartare, carpaccio and of course, ceviche. It basically means any seafood that has been marinated in citrus juice which 'cooks' the protein. Here I have used lobster but this easily works wonders with any fresh fish or other shellfish. And careful with the tequila — always warn your guests if you've added alcohol to their food in case they're driving home.

lobster ceviche with pineapple, coconut, jalapeño and mint

MAKES 20

400 g (14 oz) raw lobster tail meat
200 ml (7 fl oz) coconut cream
150 ml (5 fl oz) lime juice
60 ml (2 fl oz/¼ cup) tequila
160 g (5¾ oz/1 cup) fresh chopped
    pineapple, (cut into 1 cm (½ inch) dice)
1 tablespoon finely grated ginger
1 green jalapeño, seeded and
    finely chopped
1 small handful of mint leaves, shredded

Cut the lobster tail meat into 1 cm (½ inch) dice. Combine all the ingredients in a non-reactive bowl and season with salt and pepper. Let stand for 20 minutes to marinate. Serve in shot glasses with a small spoon or in a bowl with corn chips to scoop.

NOTE: This ceviche makes a great entrée as well as a finger food.

An empanada is basically a filled pastry or bread. They are wonderful for parties and can be made ahead of time and then just cooked to order – you can experiment with the fillings and you can search online and in books for different pastry recipes.

beef empanadas

MAKES 20

Trim and discard any sinew from the meat and dice into 1 cm (½ inch) dice, season with sea salt and pepper.

Place 120 g (4¼ oz) of the butter in a frying pan over low heat. Add the onion and cook for 8 minutes or until soft. Don't allow them to brown. Add the chilli flakes, cumin, paprika and the white part of the spring onions and cook for 15 minutes, stirring occasionally. Season with salt and pepper.

Heat the olive oil in a separate frying pan over high heat and brown the meat in two batches. Place the meat on a flat tray and allow to cool for a few minutes, then combine with the onion mixture, green part of spring onions and oregano.

To make the dough, bring 500 ml (17 fl oz/2 cups) water and the salt to boil in a small saucepan, stirring to dissolve the salt. Add the lard and stir until melted, then transfer to a large bowl. Allow to cool for 5-10 minutes.

Using your hands, gradually add 150 g (5½ oz/5½– 6 cups) flour, 1 cup at a time, until you can gather the dough in a ball. Knead the dough on a lightly-floured work surface, adding more flour until it doesn't allow anymore.

Chill the dough for an hour. Roll out half the dough at a time, on a floured work surface to 3 mm (⅛ inch) thick. Then cut into 10 cm (4 inch) rounds.

Lay a circle of dough in the palm of your hand. Place a tablespoon of the filling in the centre, leaving 6 mm (⅛ inch) border top the filling with a pinch of chopped egg, green olives and dot of the remaining butter. With your finger or a pastry brush, moisten the edges of the dough with water. Fold the dough over to enclose the filling forming a half-moon shape. Pinch the edges together and press with back of a fork to seal.

Heat some cottonseed oil in a wok or deep saucepan to 170°C (325°F). Cook the empanadas in batches, frying for 2-3 minutes each side until golden brown and crisp. Drain on kitchen paper and serve.

500 g (1 lb 2 oz) well-marbled stewing beef, such as wagyu sirloin
200 g (7 oz) unsalted butter, diced
3 onions, quartered, very thinly sliced
3 teaspoons chilli flakes
3 teaspoons ground cumin
3 teaspoons sweet Spanish smoked paprika
4 spring onions (scallions), white and green parts kept separate, chopped
2 tablespoons extra virgin olive oil
1 handful of oregano leaves, chopped
3 hard-boiled free-range eggs, coarsely chopped
60 g (2¼ oz/½ cup) pitted green olives, chopped
cottonseed oil, for deep-frying

empanada dough

1½ tablespoons salt
40 g (1½ oz) high-quality lard, diced
900 g-1.05 kg (2 lb-3 lb 5 oz/6-7 cups) plain (all-purpose) flour

I was in LA recently and the one thing I was dying to try was a fish taco. I ventured down to Hermosa Beach and walked around asking a few of the local shop owners who made the best ones. The consensus was a little shop near the beach — to the best of my recollection (as I devoured them so quickly) this is what I ate. This is now a staple recipe in my home, I make it at least once a fortnight and the kids love it.

mexican fish tacos with guacamole

MAKES 20

500 g (1 lb 2 oz) flathead fillets (or any firm, white-fleshed fish), skin and bones removed
60 g (2¼ oz) plain (all-purpose) flour
2 eggs, lightly beaten
150 g (5½ oz) cornflake crumbs
grapeseed oil, for deep-frying
20 small flour tortillas (or use large ones and cut out rounds with a 10 cm (4 inch) cutter)
2 handfuls of shredded purple cabbage or any type of lettuce
8 tablespoons sour cream or crème fraîche
4 tablespoons good-quality Mexican chilli sauce
lemon wedges, to serve

guacamole
1 avocado, finely diced
2 tomatoes, seeded and finely diced
1 bird's eye chilli, chopped
juice of 1 lime
1–2 tablespoons finely diced red onion
1 garlic clove, finely chopped
2 tablespoons chopped coriander (cilantro) leaves
1 tablespoon extra virgin olive oil

To make the guacamole, mix the avocado, tomato, chilli, lime juice, onion, garlic, coriander and olive oil together.

Cut the flathead fillets into 20 portions.

Preheat the oven to 160°C (315°F/Gas 2–3).

Put the flour in one shallow bowl, the egg in another and the cornflake crumbs in a third. Lightly season the fish with some sea salt, then dust lightly with flour, coat in the egg and then the cornflake crumbs, patting the crumbs on firmly.

Heat the grapeseed oil in a wok or deep saucepan to 160°C (315°F). Fry the fish in batches for 30–45 seconds until golden and crispy, then turn over and cook for a further 30 seconds or until cooked through. Drain on kitchen paper.

Warm the tortillas on a baking tray in the oven for 3–4 minutes. Fill the tortillas with the purple cabbage, guacamole, fish pieces, sour cream and chilli sauce. Squeeze a bit of lemon juice over the top, then put a skewer through the sides to help hold it together. Serve immediately.

The combination of squid and chorizo is a wonderful marriage (think of the Spanish paella) and a great way of having surf and turf at your next party. This is a simple, lovely recipe that will get the tastebuds jumping. You could also substitute the squid for cuttlefish, scallops or any type of fish if you wish.

ancho-spiced squid and chorizo brocheta with chipotle aïoli

MAKES 20

Soak the bamboo skewers in water for 1 hour.

Remove the skin from the squid and take out the cartilage from the inside. Cut open the squid lengthways, score the inside surface of the squid and cut into rectangular pieces about 4 cm (1½ inches) long.

Thread the chorizo and squid onto the skewers, so the chorizo sits inside the piece of squid.

To make the aïoli, place the egg yolks in a mixing bowl (or you could use a food processor), add garlic and lemon juice and whisk to combine. Continue to whisk, slowly pouring in the oil until the aïoli is creamy. Season with salt and the chipotle chilli.

Heat the vegetable oil in a wok or deep saucepan to 180°C (350°F).

Mix together the tapioca flour and the spices and coat each skewer in the seasoned flour. To cook, carefully place the skewers a few at a time in the oil and cook for 2 minutes until crisp and golden. Drain on kitchen paper and serve with the aïoli.

NOTE: Ancho chilli – is a large, dried poblano chilli. Dark purple to black in colour and mildly fruity in flavour with subtle coffee notes, it is used in traditional Mexican dishes. Chipotle chilli is a delicious smoked, dried jalapeno.

brocheta
300 g (10½ oz) small squid tubes
4 chorizo, sliced on an angle
vegetable oil, for frying
400 g (14 oz) tapioca flour
2 tablespoons ground ancho chilli
1 tablespoon cracked black pepper
2 tablespoons paprika

aïoli
5 free-range egg yolks
1 garlic clove, crushed
juice of 3 lemons
300 ml (10½ fl oz) extra virgin olive oil
1 teaspoon ground chipotle chilli

mexican punch

SERVES 4

Place all the ingredients in a small punch bowl or large carafe over ice. Once chilled serve in old fashioned glasses, garnished with fresh fruit and mint sprigs.

180 ml (6 fl oz) Tequila Reposado
60 ml (2 fl oz/¼ cup) Grand Marnier
120 ml (4 fl oz) orange juice
120 ml (4 fl oz) pineapple juice
8 blood orange slices
3 tablespoons pomegranate seeds
12 mint leaves
40 ml (1¼ fl oz) lemon juice
fresh fruit and 6 mint sprigs, to garnish

tommy's margarita

SERVES 1

Use the lime wedge to run over the rim of an old fashioned glass. Half rim the glass with the salt. Place all the ingredients in a shaker over ice. Shake and then strain into the glass filled with ice. Garnish with the lime zest.

NOTE: Named in honour of Tommy Bermejo of the world's leading tequila family.

1 lime wedge
signature salt (see page 241)
30 ml (1 fl oz) Tequila Blanco
30 ml (1 fl oz) lime juice
15 ml (½ fl oz) agave nectar (agave syrup)
zest of 1 lime, to garnish

in bloom

SERVES 1

30 ml (1 fl oz) Tequila Reposado
60 ml (2 fl oz/¼ cup) grapefruit juice
dash of grapefruit bitters
   (Fee Bros works well)
30 ml (1 fl oz) Massenez Camomile liqueur
1 teaspoon of orange marmalade
soda water
1 peach slice, to garnish

Place all the ingredients in a highball glass (except the soda water) over ice and stir. Top up with soda water. Garnish with a slice of peach.

little pj

SERVES 1

1 orange wedge
combined orange sugar and cinnamon
   sugar (see page 242)
60 ml (2 fl oz/¼ cup) Tequila
   (Anejo works well)
10 ml (2 teaspoons) Noilly Prat
10 ml (2 teaspoons) agave nectar
   (agave syrup)
dash of orange bitters (Regan's works well)

Use the orange wedge to run around the rim of an old fashioned glass. Half rim the glass with the combined sugars. Stir the remaining ingredients in a martini pitcher over ice. Strain with a julep strainer into the glass filled with ice.

smoky cadillac

SERVES 1

4 chargrilled lime wedges (see note)
45 ml (1½ fl oz) Mezcal
15 ml (½ fl oz) Grand Marnier
15 ml (½ fl oz) pineapple juice
dash of sugar syrup (see page 238)
pineapple crisp (see page 241) with
    cinnamon sugar (see page 242),
    to garnish

Add the lime wedges to a shaker and press to release the juice. Then add the remaining ingredients to the shaker over ice. Shake and double strain into a chilled martini glass and garnish with the pineapple crisp and cinnamon sugar.

NOTE: Cut a lime into wedges and then cook the wedges on a preheated grill for 2–3 minutes or until nicely chargrilled. This adds a smoked flavour to the drink.

coming of age

SERVES 1

2 grapefruit zests
30 ml (1 fl oz) Tequila Anejo
30 ml (1 fl oz) Oloroso Sherry (Seppeltsfield
    works well)
10 ml (2 teaspoons) grenadine
10 ml (2 teaspoons) Massenez clear
    ginger liqueur (or ginger syrup,
    see page 239)

Pre-stain the martini glass with 1 grapefruit zest and discard, then place all the ingredients in a glass Boston shaker over cubed ice. Stir 16 times and strain all the ingredients into the glass with a julep strainer. Garnish with the remaining grapefruit zest twisted into the drink.

silver lining

SERVES 1

Place all the ingredients in a shaker, dry shake (with no ice), then add the ice and shake vigorously to emulsify the egg white. Pour into a chilled martini glass. Garnish with the cucumber flower.

45 ml (1½ fl oz) Tequila Blanco
30 ml (1 fl oz) sweetened aloe vera water
   (available at health food stores)
15 ml (½ fl oz) lime juice
15 ml (½ fl oz) sugar syrup (see page 238)
dash of egg white
cucumber flower, to garnish

sangrita

SERVES 1

Serve the tequila in a spirit glass. Combine the orange and tomato juice, Tabasco and chilli flakes and serve in another spirit glass. Serve as a tasting flight, so you can sip the tequila then sip the spiced juice, with the lime wedge on the side.

30 ml (1 fl oz) tequila
20 ml (½ fl oz) tomato juice
20 ml (½ fl oz) orange juice
6 drops Tabasco
pinch of chilli flakes
lime wedge, to serve

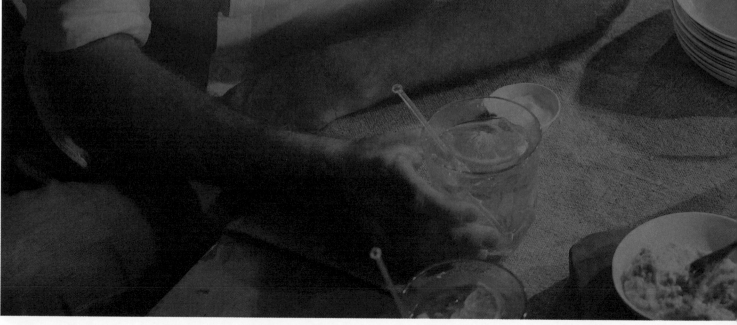

supper club

Supper clubs are becoming increasingly popular and that's a good thing.
In this chapter I have created slightly more substantial versions of the
canapé to be served midway through your party to help line the stomach.
Each and every drink in this section holds a story and element of elegance
only truly appreciated at night.

This is a wonderful way to use leftover risotto from the night before or if you are purpose-making these, you can put anything you like in the arancini (risotto balls) that takes your fancy. Basically any type of risotto you love makes for a great arancini. The reason I love this one is that it is my favourite type of risotto to make at home — full of flavour and visually stunning. It gets even better when you make the arancini as the outside crust gives a great contrast and serving lemon wedges on the side makes them look so attractive to gobble down.

spinach and taleggio arancini

MAKES 20

1 bunch English spinach, washed and trimmed (picked weight of about 125 g/4½ oz)
150 g (5½ oz) unsalted butter, softened
200 ml (7 fl oz) vegetable stock or water
2 teaspoons vegetable oil
2 garlic cloves, finely chopped
½ small white onion, finely chopped
110 g (3¾ oz/½ cup) arborio rice
50 ml (1½ fl oz) white wine
3 tablespoons chopped flat-leaf (Italian) parsley
70 g (2½ oz) taleggio cheese, cut into 1 cm (¼ inch) cubes
2 tablespoons grated parmesan cheese
2 eggs
plain (all-purpose) flour, for dusting
100 g (3½ oz/1 cup) dry breadcrumbs
vegetable oil, for deep-frying
lemon wedges and aïoli (see page 112), to serve (optional)

Make a spinach purée by blanching the leaves for 10 seconds in boiling salted water. Drain and then squeeze out the excess liquid while still hot. Process in a blender with the butter until emulsified into a rich smooth purée.

Heat the stock in a saucepan over medium heat to just below simmering.

Heat the oil in a separate small heavy-based saucepan over medium-low heat and cook the garlic and onion until softened and translucent. Add the rice and cook for 30 seconds, stirring well to coat all the grains with the oil. Add the wine and cook out the alcohol for a further 30 seconds. Add the hot stock and stir. Turn down the heat and simmer for 15 minutes, stirring often, until just cooked.

Remove from the heat and fold through the spinach and parsley. Season with salt and pepper.

Then fold in the taleggio and parmesan cheese. Spread onto a tray and allow to cool.

Once the risotto is completely cool, roll 3 teaspoons of the mix into balls and place into the refrigerator for 10 minutes or until firm.

Whisk the eggs in a bowl with 50 ml (1½ fl oz) of water to make an egg wash. Place some flour into one bowl and the breadcrumbs into another bowl.

Dust the rice balls with flour, dip them in the egg mix, then coat with the crumbs.

Heat the vegetable oil to 180°C (350°F) in a wok or deep frying pan. Deep-fry the arancini in batches for 3 minutes or until golden brown and crisp, drain on kitchen paper. Season with sea salt and serve with lemon wedges and aïoli, if desired.

I'd just completed my culinary duties for G'Day USA — an American/
Australian art and culture promotion in New York, when I met up
with Monica Duggan at the Consulate-General of Australia's
farewell do. After a glass or two of fine champagne, Monica let me
in on her family's secret recipe to making borscht — since then she
has cooked it for me and it is wonderful. It rightly deserves a place
in this book. Thanks Monica, I owe you one!

monica's beetroot borscht with crème fraîche and dill

SERVES 20

Place the bone marrow in a large saucepan with 1 litre (35 fl oz/4 cups) water, bay
leaf and some salt to make a stock. Simmer for 30 minutes, skimming
occasionally, and then strain.

Return the stock to medium heat, add the cabbage, bring to the boil, then add
the potato and carrot then simmer partly covered for 30 minutes.

Meanwhile, in a separate saucepan, melt the butter over low heat, add the onion
and garlic and cook until just translucent. Add the beetroot, red wine vinegar,
sugar, tomatoes and a little salt and pepper. Add the celeriac, parsnip and turnip.
Pour in the marrow stock and cabbage and gently simmer until all the vegetables
are tender. Do not boil as the soup will lose its colour. Serve in small bowls topped
with a spoonful of crème fraîche and dill sprigs.

1 kg (2 lb 4 oz) bone marrow
1 bay leaf
½ small white cabbage, shredded
1 small potato, diced
1 carrot, finely diced
20 g (¾ oz) butter
½ onion, finely chopped
2 garlic cloves, chopped
1 bunch large beetroot, peeled and
    finely shredded
2½ tablespoons red wine vinegar
½ teaspoon sugar
125 g (4½ oz) tinned chopped tomatoes
½ small celeriac, finely diced
½ parsnip, finely diced
½ turnip, finely diced
80 g (2¾ oz/⅓ cup) crème fraîche,
    to serve
dill sprigs, to serve

This dish is inspired from travelling through South-East Asia and tasting all the amazing soups they sell on the side of the road, at markets and restaurants. Generally when you eat these soups overseas you don't know which part of the animal you're eating and sometimes you are much better off not asking. I've chosen oxtail as it has a wonderful flavour and is an under-utilised and often misunderstood ingredient. If you don't fancy the idea of eating tail, then you can use any other secondary cut of beef such as shin, cheek or any part you would put in a stew.

braised oxtail dumplings with mushroom broth

SERVES 20

3 kg (6 lb 12 oz) oxtail (ask your butcher
to cut it into 5 cm (2 inch) pieces)
2 tablespoons vegetable oil
6 coriander (cilantro) roots, washed and
roughly chopped
5 garlic cloves
1 large knob ginger, chopped
10 white peppercorns
1 red onion, diced
2½ tablespoons sugar
100 ml (3½ fl oz) oyster sauce
30 ml (1 fl oz) Chinese black vinegar
3 litres (105 fl oz/12 cups) chicken stock
60 gow gee wrappers
15 oyster mushrooms, torn into 4 pieces
1 large handful of mint leaves,
finely shredded
1 large handful of coriander
(cilantro) leaves
1 large handful of Vietnamese mint leaves
6 spring onions (scallions),
finely shredded
juice of 2 limes
pinch of hot chilli powder,
to serve (optional)

Preheat the oven to 200°C (400°F/Gas 6). Roast the oxtail in a heavy-based roasting tin drizzled with some oil for 30 minutes.

Pound the coriander roots with the garlic, ginger, white peppercorns and a pinch of salt to form a paste.

Heat a small amount of the vegetable oil in a large heavy-based saucepan and fry the paste with the onion over a medium heat for 5–10 minutes stirring continuously until it begins to caramelise.

Next add the sugar, oyster sauce, Chinese black vinegar, chicken stock and the pieces of oxtail. Bring to a simmer and cover the surface with some non-stick baking paper and seal with foil or cover with a lid.

Braise the oxtail for 3–3½ hours or until soft and falling off the bone. Remove the pieces of oxtail from the stock.

Strain the liquid twice through a fine sieve, allow to cool slightly, skim off the fat and set aside. Remove the meat from the bones, discard any fat and finely chop the oxtail.

Place a gow gee wrapper on a clean work surface. Place 1 heaped teaspoonful of oxtail filling in the centre of the wrapper. Brush the edges of the wrapper lightly with a little water. Fold the wrapper over to enclose the filling and form a half-moon shape. Repeat with the remaining gow gee and filling.

To finish the dish, bring the stock to the boil, turn down to a simmer and add the torn mushrooms. Blanch the dumplings in plenty of salted boiling water. Serve 3 gow gees per person in a small bowl with a little of the broth, some oyster mushroom and some of the mint, coriander, Vietnamese mint and spring onion on top. Drizzle with some lime juice and sprinkle with the hot chilli powder.

When you order this in Italy, you generally get poached veal slices coated in a gorgeous tuna mayonnaise with capers. It is such a lovely dish but can be somewhat overbearing if you eat too much of it. That is why I love to serve it in its miniature form as a canapé. It fits any type of occasion — you can either dress it down for a casual get-together or dress it up with the addition of some fried capers, preserved lemon and baby herbs to really give it some sophistication.

vitello tonnato

MAKES 20

Preheat the oven to 160°C (315°F/Gas 2–3). To make the croutons slice the sourdough into 5 mm (¼ inch) thick slices and lay on baking trays. Drizzle with olive oil, season with sea salt and cook for 5 minutes or until golden brown.

Reduce the oven temperature to 140°C (275°F/Gas 1). Heat a frying pan with a touch of olive oil and sear the veal fillet on all sides until golden. Place on a baking tray and cook in the oven for about 10 minutes or until rare–medium-rare and then take out of the oven and rest for 20 minutes.

To make the crispy garlic, put the garlic and oil in a saucepan and heat until the garlic starts to turn golden. Lift out the garlic with a slotted spoon and drain on kitchen paper.

Mix together the tuna, aïoli, capers, anchovies, parsley, lemon zest and season with salt and pepper.

Slice the veal thinly. Spread some of the tuna and caper aïoli onto the crouton, top with a slice of veal and garnish with the crispy garlic, baby herbs dressed in lemon juice and extra capers.

1 day-old sourdough loaf

400 g (14 oz) veal fillet

100 g (3½ oz) tinned tuna in olive oil, drained and roughly chopped

8 tablespoons aïoli (see page 112, omit the chipotle chilli)

3 teaspoons salted capers, rinsed

3 anchovies, chopped

1 tablespoon chopped flat-leaf (Italian) parsley

zest of 1 lemon or 1 tablespoon preserved lemon, finely shredded

baby herbs or watercress sprigs, to serve

squeeze of lemon juice, to serve

extra salted capers, rinsed, to serve

crispy garlic

4 garlic cloves, thinly sliced

250 ml (9 fl oz/1 cup) vegetable oil

This is the pizza I'm most proud of creating. It came about from one of the entrees I used to serve at Hugos Bondi — it was asparagus with egg yolk ravioli and brown butter sauce. I loved the flavours and presentation and I really wanted to create an asparagus pizza for the vegetarians. I toyed around with 50 or so versions of this pizza before finally settling upon the one presented here. It isn't our most popular as you can imagine (try competing against pepperoni or margherita) but I think it's the one that attracts the most compliments. I just love the texture of the runny egg and the crunchy walnuts.

asparagus pizza with truffle and egg

MAKES 4 X 30 CM (12 INCH) PIZZAS

To make the pizza dough, put the yeast, sugar, salt and olive oil in a mixing bowl with 250 ml (9 fl oz/1 cup) of warm water and stir gently. Leave for 15 minutes for the yeast to activate (it will look foamy). Add the flour slowly and knead for about 5 minutes until the dough is smooth.

Place the dough in a lightly-oiled bowl and leave to sit in a warm place, covered until doubled in size, then knock back with one good punch. Leave in a warm place until it has risen slightly.

To make the roast garlic, preheat the oven to 180°C (350°F/Gas 4). Separate the garlic cloves leaving them unpeeled. Place on a sheet of foil, drizzle with the olive oil and seal the foil. Cook on a baking tray lined with some rock salt for 15–20 minutes or until soft and golden. Cool slightly and remove the cloves, discarding the skins.

Preheat your oven to its highest temperature. Weigh 4 x 170 g (6 oz) balls of pizza dough. Using a rolling pin, roll out each portion on a work bench dusted with either semolina or flour. Lift each dough base onto a 30 cm (12 inch) pizza tray. Prick the bases all over with a fork to stop air bubbles forming when they are cooking. Brush each pizza with some extra virgin olive oil, then spread with the goat's curd, top with mozzarella, roasted garlic, parsley and asparagus.

Crack an egg into the centre of each pizza and then top the egg with a little of the grated parmesan.

Season with salt and pepper.

Bake in the oven for 5–10 minutes or until golden and crispy. Top with the shaved parmesan, toasted walnuts and the truffle oil.

1 quantity pizza dough (see recipe below)
semolina, for rolling (optional)
extra virgin olive oil
160 g (5¾ oz) goat's curd
120 g (4¼ oz) shredded mozzarella
4 roasted garlic cloves, chopped
1 tablespoon chopped parsley
24 blanched asparagus spears, cut in
    half lengthways
4 free-range eggs
4 tablespoons grated parmesan
shaved parmesan, to serve
4 tablespoons crushed, toasted walnuts
1 tablespoon white truffle oil

pizza dough

3 teaspoons active dried yeast
3 teaspoons sugar
3 teaspoons salt
1 tablespoon olive oil
425 g (15 oz) 00 flour

roasted garlic

1 bulb of garlic
2 tablespoons olive oil
rock salt

Kaz Derbas is my pizza chef at Hugos Manly and has been with me since the day we opened. Every day he is there with a smile and a laugh for everyone — I have never worked with a person who brings such joy to a kitchen. That said, he is also a true artisan of pizza making. This is the pizza he created for a prestigious pizza competition held each year in Australia and which took out first place. Well done Kaz and thanks for another delicious offering.

hiramasa kingfish pizza with artichoke purée and pomegranate

MAKES 4 X 30 CM (12 INCH) PIZZAS

1 small eggplant (aubergine)
oil, for deep-frying
3 tablespoons black peppercorns
2 tablespoons coriander seeds
2 tablespoons yellow mustard seeds
320 g (11¼ oz) kingfish fillet, skin removed
3 tablespoons vegetable oil
1 quantity pizza dough
    (see recipe opposite)
semolina, for rolling (optional)
2 tablespoons chopped oregano
120 g (4¼ oz) shredded mozzarella
1 pomegranate, seeds removed
1 tablespoon pomegranate molasses
baby watercress, to serve

saffron onions

3 tablespoons white wine
1 teaspoon white vinegar
pinch of saffron threads
½ teaspoon white sugar
1 small white onion, thinly sliced

artichoke purée

250 g (9 oz) jar artichoke hearts in
    olive oil, drained
4 roasted garlic cloves
    (see recipe opposite)
2 tablespoons olive oil

To make the saffron onions, combine the wine, vinegar and saffron threads in a small saucepan over low heat and cook for 2 minutes, then add the sugar and onion. Increase the heat to medium and stir gently. Cook for 10 minutes then set aside.

To make the artichoke purée, combine the artichokes with the garlic and oil using a hand blender until smooth, season with salt.

Cut the eggplant into quarters and with a sharp knife remove the seeds then dice into 2 cm (¾ inch) pieces. Heat the oil to 160°C (315°F) in a wok or deep saucepan. Deep-fry the eggplant in batches for 2 minutes or until golden. Remove with a slotted spoon and drain on kitchen paper.

Roast the peppercorns, the coriander and mustard seeds in a small frying pan over medium–high heat until fragrant. Place in a spice grinder or use a mortar and pestle and grind to a fine powder. Cut the kingfish into 4 x 80 g (2¾ oz) pieces. Coat the kingfish with 1 tablespoon of the vegetable oil, then evenly coat with the spice mix.

Preheat your oven to its highest temperature. Weigh 4 x 170 g (6 oz) balls of pizza dough. Using a rolling pin, roll out each portion on a work bench dusted with either semolina or flour. Lift each dough base onto a 30 cm (12 inch) pizza tray and prick the bases all over with a fork to stop air bubbles forming when they are cooking. Spread 3 tablespoons of the artichoke purée onto each pizza base and then top with saffron onions, deep-fried eggplant, oregano and the mozzarella. Cook for 5–10 minutes or until golden and crispy.

Meanwhile, heat the remaining oil in a non-stick frying pan over high heat. Sear the kingfish for 15 seconds on each side and allow to rest, then slice the kingfish into 5 mm (¼ inch) thick slices.

To finish, sprinkle the pomegranate seeds all over, place the kingfish on top and drizzle with the pomegranate molasses then scatter over the baby watercress.

My first book, *Fish*, had my recipe for paella in it and I've never had more comments about a recipe from people saying how much they loved making it for their family and friends. So naturally, I had to include a paella recipe for entertaining in this book. I've simplified it by just putting in two proteins — the chorizo, which everyone loves and one of my favourite seafood items, the vongole or sand cockle. I love these little morsels because they are the ultimate finger food that should be slurped out of their shell with as much noise as possible but only when you're with very close friends and family of course.

chorizo and clam paella

SERVES 20

Preheat the oven to 180°C (350°F/Gas 4). Put the stock in a saucepan over medium–low heat and add half the lemon and the saffron threads.

Heat a touch of oil in a frying pan and cook the garlic, tomatoes and paprika for a few minutes until soft, then purée with a blender or a mortar and pestle. (This mixture is called picada.)

Heat the oil in a paella pan or large heavy-based frying pan and cook the chorizo on both sides. Add the rice and the picada and cook for a few minutes, stirring well.

Strain the hot stock into the paella pan and stir well. Add a touch of sea salt, bring to the boil for 5 minutes and then stir again.

Add the vongole to the paella pan, cover with a lid or foil and put in the oven for 15–20 minutes, or until the rice is cooked and the vongole have opened. Discard any that have not opened. Arrange the pimento or capsicum strips over the top with the chopped parsley and lemon zest. Season with sea salt and cracked pepper if needed, spoon into small bowls, squeeze over the remaining lemon and serve immediately.

1.5 litres (52 fl oz/6 cups) fish or
   chicken stock
2 lemons, zested and then cut in half
¼ teaspoon saffron threads
4 garlic cloves, crushed
4 ripe tomatoes, chopped
2 teaspoons smoked paprika (I like to use
   La Chinata)
80 ml (2½ fl oz/⅓ cup) extra virgin olive oil
2 chorizo sausages, cut into 1 cm
   (½ inch) slices
500 g (1 lb 2 oz) Calasparra or Bomba
   short-grain white rice
1 kg (2 lb 4 oz) vongole (sand cockle)
150 g (5½ oz) pimentos or roasted
   capsicum (pepper), cut into strips
large handful of flat-leaf (Italian) parsley

The biggest seller at all of my restaurants is always any squid, calamari or cuttlefish dish, served as a starter and deep-fried to perfection. As a chef, you want the dishes you create to be unique, jump off the menu and become a hit with your customers. It is the unwritten law though that the most common thing will always sell more than something someone is a bit unsure of. This is one sure way to have the majority of people at your next party think you're amazing. I've never met anyone that doesn't like fried squid, me included.

sichuan spiced crispy squid with mouth-numbing sauce

SERVES 20

500 g (1 lb 2 oz) squid tubes
75 g (2½ oz/½ cup) plain
   (all-purpose) flour
35 g (1¼ oz) rice flour
1 tablespoon salt, plus extra to serve
1 tablespoon roasted and ground sichuan
   pepper, plus extra to serve
1 tablespoon ground white pepper
2 egg whites
canola oil, for deep frying
lime wedges, to serve

mouth-numbing sauce
1 tablespoon roasted and ground
   sichuan pepper
juice of 4 limes

Remove the skin from the squid and take out the cartilage from the inside. Cut open the squid lengthways and then score the inside surface. Cut the squid into thin strips about 4 mm (¼ inch) thick.

To make the mouth-numbing sauce, combine the sichuan pepper and lime juice.

Combine plain flour, rice flour, salt, sichuan pepper and white pepper in a large bowl. Beat the egg whites and lightly coat the squid in the egg whites and then dust with the flour mixture. Shake off any excess flour.

Heat the canola oil to 185°C (350°F) in a large, deep saucepan or wok. When hot, cook the squid in small batches (so the oil stays hot and the squid gets crunchy) briefly until light golden in colour. Drain on kitchen paper, season with extra sichuan pepper and salt and serve in paper cones with lime wedges and the mouth-numbing sauce.

People always like to have a substantial item on the menu for when the finger-foods have disappeared. I like to offer a pasta or a rice dish as I find people can really relate to it as comfort food and can then relax into the party. This recipe is very easy to make and you can adapt it for vegetarians as well. When thinking about serving pasta for numerous people always try to remember to use short pasta such as penne, orecchiette, rigatoni and gnocchi. It's easier for people to eat and they also have much less chance of spilling it on themselves. This is my executive chef, Massimo Mele's recipe and of course it works just as well as a main course.

rigatoni with prawn, spinach and pesto

SERVES 20

To make the pesto, using either a mortar and pestle or hand-held blender, start with the garlic and some salt, pound these together until they have broken down to a paste then add the pine nuts and pound them to a paste before adding the anchovies.

Next add the basil and when that has been pounded to a paste add the cheese (we won't add as much for a normal pesto as we are matching this with seafood) then the lemon zest, lemon juice and the olive oil until you have a sauce consistency. Season with cracked black pepper and more salt if needed.

Heat the olive oil in a large deep frying pan over high heat. Add the prawns and cook until golden on one side, turn them over and cook until almost done, then add the garlic, chilli and wine and set aside.

Meanwhile, cook the rigatoni in a large saucepan of boiling salted water until al dente. Drain, reserving the pasta cooking water, then add the rigatoni to the prawns with about 1 cup of the pasta water. Add the spinach, pesto and enough lemon juice to taste (you might not need it all.)

Stir until well combined, season with salt and cracked pepper to taste, and serve.

pesto

10 roasted garlic cloves (see page 132)
60 g (2¼ oz) toasted pine nuts
2 anchovies
200 g (7 oz/4 cups) picked basil leaves
2 tablespoons grated parmesan
zest of 2 lemons
juice of 2 lemons
60 ml (2 fl oz/¼ cup) olive oil

2 tablespoons olive oil
20 green king prawns (shrimp), peeled and deveined, tails intact
2 garlic cloves, sliced
2 red chillies, seeded and sliced
100 ml (3½ fl oz) white wine
800 g (1 lb 12 oz) rigatoni
200 g (7 oz) baby spinach
juice of 2 lemons

negroni

SERVES 1

1 orange twist
rough shards of ice
30 ml (1 fl oz) gin (a London Dry varietal
 works well)
30 ml (1 fl oz) Cinzano Rosso
30 ml (1 fl oz) Campari
extra orange twist, to garnish
soda water (optional)

Pre-stain an old fashioned glass with an orange twist then discard. Add the rough shards of ice. Add the remaining ingredients, stir and then add more ice and garnish with the fresh orange twist. You can serve soda on the side if you like.

gentleman's digestif

SERVES 1

30 ml (1 fl oz) Amaro Montenegro
orange wedge, to garnish
45 ml (1½ fl oz) blood orange or
 mandarin sorbet
5 ml (1 teaspoon) lemon juice
30 ml (1 fl oz) Prosecco

Serve the Amaro Montenegro over ice in an old fashioned glass, garnished with the orange wedge. Mix the sorbet, lemon juice and Prosecco in a mixing glass to combine. Then serve on the side in a champagne saucer or tasting glass as a palate cleanser.

martinez

SERVES 1

Place all the ingredients into a shaker over ice. Shake and then strain into a chilled martini glass. Garnish with the maraschino cherry.

45 ml (1½ fl oz) gin
15 ml (½ fl oz) Noilly Prat
dash of maraschino liqueur
dash of Angostura bitters
dash of sugar syrup (see page 238)
maraschino cherry, to garnish

blood and sand

SERVES 4

Place all the ingredients into a jug and stir. Serve in martini glasses straight up. Garnish each drink by flaming the orange zests.

80 ml (2½ fl oz/⅓ cup) single malt whisky
80 ml (2½ fl oz/⅓ cup) Cinzano Rosso
80 ml (2½ fl oz/⅓ cup) cherry brandy
120 ml (4 fl oz) orange juice
4 x 3 x 6 cm (1¼ x 2½ inch) flamed
orange zests, to garnish (see page 242)

manhattan

SERVES 1

60 ml (2 fl oz) rye whisky
   (Jim Beam Rye works well)
15 ml (½ fl oz) sweet vermouth
dash of Angostura bitters
dash of maraschino cherry juice
maraschino cherry, to garnish

Place all the ingredients into a martini pitcher (or in a shaker if you like it more diluted). Stir over ice, then strain into a chilled martini glass (or an old fashioned glass if served on the rocks) and garnish with the maraschino cherry.

old fashioned

SERVES 1

60 ml (2 fl oz/¼ cup) bourbon
10 ml (2 teaspoons) brown sugar syrup
   (see page 239)
dash of Angostura bitters
1 orange zest, 1 lemon zest and
   a maraschino cherry, to garnish

Place the bourbon, syrup and bitters into an old fashioned glass, then stir 10 times. Add some ice and stir 6 times. Garnish with the orange zest, lemon zest and a cherry. Top with fresh ice.

flame of love

SERVES 1

Flame the zests into a martini glass, then discard the zests. Shake the remaining ingredients over ice into a boston shaker and strain into the martini glass, garnish with a floating orange crisp.

NOTE: This cocktail was inspired by 'King of Cocktails' — Dale Degroff.

2 flamed orange zests (see page 242)
2 flamed lemon zests (see page 242)
60 ml (2 fl oz/¼ cup) vodka
15 ml (½ fl oz) Oloroso sherry
orange crisps (see page 241), to garnish
3 drops Angostura bitters (optional)

mint julep

SERVES 4

Place all the ingredients into a shaker over ice. Shake and then strain into a glass filled with crushed ice. Garnish with the mint sprig.

NOTE: To make 240 ml (8 fl oz) of mint-infused rye bourbon, add 280 ml (10 fl oz) of bourbon to a bowl and then add the leaves from 4 mint sprigs to the bowl and let it sit for 2 hours to flavour. Then squeeze the bourbon out of the mint and add back to the bottle to use for a mint julep.

240 ml (8 fl oz) rye bourbon
24 mint leaves
60 ml (2 fl oz/¼ cup) sugar syrup
   (see page 238)
mint sprigs, to garnish
3 drops Angostura bitters (optional)

chill factor

As the weather cools we like to find comfort in our meals as much as our knitted socks and woollen blankets. Warm yourself by an open fire in a ski chalet or your own cosy lounge with spicy mulled wine or a bourbon toddy. This is food for the soul.

This will be a firm favourite at your next party when you want to warm up the crowd. It is such a simple recipe but it uses a few spectacular ingredients — figs, prosciutto and the king of Italian cheese, gorgonzola. This also makes a great entrée if you serve two of them with a bit of crunchy sourdough on the side to mop up the leftover sauce ... yummo!

baked figs with gorgonzola sauce

SERVES 20

20 thin prosciutto slices (San Daniele preferably)
5 figs, cut into quarters
30 g (1 oz) butter, softened
400 ml (14 fl oz) cream
250 g (9 oz) gorgonzola, chopped
finely shredded basil or other baby herbs, to serve

Preheat the oven to 200°C (400°F/Gas 6).

Wrap one slice of prosciutto around the middle of each piece of fig and secure with a toothpick.

Place the butter, cream and gorgonzola together in a saucepan over low heat, stirring to create a sauce with some pieces of gorgonzola still visible. Place the figs in an ovenproof dish, pour the sauce over and cover the dish with foil. Bake in the oven for 7 minutes, remove the foil and bake for 1 minute more.

Place each fig in a small bowl, remove the toothpick and spoon a little of the sauce over, then top with the herbs. Serve immediately.

This recipe featured in my first cookbook and TV show titled *Fish* and it is still one of the easiest and tastiest finger-food recipes I love to make. It was inspired by my first trip to Thailand and the first dish I tried in Bangkok. I can't tell you how many times I've made it since but I never tire of the process or the taste and neither will you. You can serve and steam this in shot glasses, banana leaves or small bowls.

steamed fish curry with crispy shallots

SERVES 20

To make the crispy shallots, place the shallots and oil in a saucepan and heat until the shallots start to turn golden. Lift out the shallots with a slotted spoon and drain on kitchen paper.

Finely dice the fish and place in a chilled bowl. Whisk together the eggs, coconut milk, fish sauce, palm sugar, curry paste, kaffir lime leaf, chilli, mint and lime juice and then stir through the diced fish.

Spoon the fish mixture into 20 small Chinese bowls with a few leaves of Thai basil. Cover with plastic wrap.

To cook the fish curries, place a few bowls at a time in a large steamer over simmering water and steam for about 5–8 minutes or until the fish is cooked through (carefully open one to check — it should look like a just-set custard). Serve with extra Thai basil, crispy shallots, chilli and lime wedges.

400 g (14 oz) white-fleshed fish (such as snapper, mullet, barramundi, bream, trevally)
4 free-range eggs
250 ml (9 fl oz/1 cup) coconut milk
2 tablespoons fish sauce
2 tablespoons grated palm sugar (jaggery)
3–4 teaspoons red curry paste
10 kaffir lime leaves, finely sliced
2 chillies, finely chopped
10 mint leaves, finely sliced
juice of 2 limes
2 large handfuls of Thai basil or coriander (cilantro) leaves, plus extra to serve
crispy shallots, to serve
extra chillies, seeded and finely sliced, to serve
lime wedges, to serve

crispy shallots
4 French shallots (eschalots), thinly sliced
500 ml (17 fl oz/2 cups) vegetable oil

I've never witnessed such love for a vegetable as I have when watching people attack a platter of fried zucchini flowers. I know if I put out a platter of fried zucchini pieces the reception wouldn't be half as much. This is a classic recipe with some cheese and a salty anchovy inserted inside the flower to add a bit of colour and flavour. You can fry the flowers with nothing inside but it is nice to have a surprise when you bite into them.

fried zucchini flowers, buffalo mozzarella, anchovy and crispy mint

MAKES 20

tempura batter

200 g (7 oz) tempura flour
350 ml (12 fl oz) ice-cold sparkling
    mineral water

20 zucchini (courgette) flowers
2 balls of Italian buffalo mozzarella, each
    torn into 4 pieces
10 small good-quality anchovies, chopped
vegetable oil, for deep-frying
1 large handful of mint leaves
plain (all-purpose) flour, for dusting
½ teaspoon chilli flakes
lemon wedges, to serve

To make the tempura batter, put the tempura flour in a mixing bowl and slowly pour in the mineral water while you whisk. Continue whisking until the batter has the consistency of pouring cream.

Inside the zucchini flower is the stamen (male) or pistils (female), remove these with tweezers or with your fingers (not really necessary but it tastes better if you do this).

Place a piece of buffalo mozzarella and a small amount of anchovies inside each flower and twist at the end to seal.

Heat the oil to 180°C (350°F) in a wok or deep pan. Fry the mint leaves in batches in the oil until crisp and remove with a slotted spoon. Lightly dust the flowers in flour and shake off any excess. Dip in the tempura batter and drain off the excess. Deep-fry for about 2 minutes until the flowers are lightly golden and crisp. Drain on kitchen paper and sprinkle with sea salt.

Scatter the mint leaves on top of the flowers with chilli flakes and serve with the lemon wedges.

This is a recipe that was inspired by arguably Australia's finest culinary ambassador, Neil Perry. I can remember my first visit to Rockpool about 15 years ago and this was the canapé that was served to me. Wow, what a taste sensation! This was how I wanted my food to look and taste. The next day I bought Neil's cookbook and studied each and every recipe. I have taken the liberty of simplifying the pasta recipe by using gow gee wrappers (which you can pick up in the frozen section of your supermarket or Asian grocer).

goat's curd tortellini with brown butter and muscatel raisins

MAKES 20

Combine the goat's curd, chives, lemon zest, salt and white pepper for the goat's curd filling. Place 1 teaspoon of filling in the centre of each gow gee wrapper and brush a little water around the edges. Fold over into a half-moon shape and join two corners together to form a tortellini, press to seal.

Heat the butter in a frying pan for 2–3 minutes or until it turns nut brown. Add the balsamic vinegar and then the pine nuts, sage, muscatels and some salt and pepper.

Cook the tortellini in boiling salted water for about 2 minutes or until cooked through, then lift out with a slotted spoon. Add the tortellini to the butter mixture, toss gently and sprinkle with the parmesan and serve.

200 g (7 oz) goat's curd
1 bunch chives, finely snipped
zest of 2 lemons
20 gow gee wrappers
100 g (3½ oz) butter
25 ml (1¼ fl oz) balsamic vinegar
1 tablespoon pine nuts
2 teaspoons chopped sage
30 g (1 oz/¼ cup) muscatels
3 tablespoons finely
 grated parmesan

When my business partners and I first opened our Melbourne restaurant The Pantry about 20 years ago, I made sausage rolls every day and had them on the menu – they were huge sellers and I loved making them. These days they don't feature on the menu but they do often feature when I do catering – everyone loves them and you can jazz them up a bit with some homemade tomato sauce or relish or chutney so they have a bit more class!

pork and fennel sausage rolls

MAKES 36

Preheat the oven to 200°C (400°F/Gas 6). Toast the fennel seeds in a hot frying pan with the peppercorns for 1 minute, tossing regularly until fragrant. Place in a mortar and pestle with a pinch of sea salt and the nutmeg and grind, to break up the seeds.

Combine the pork mince with the vegetables and then mix through the spices. Season with plenty of salt and cracked black pepper.

Divide each sheet of puff pastry evenly into 3 strips. Divide the pork mixture into 9 equal portions. Add the pork mince to the long side of each strip in a straight line leaving a lip of pastry which will seal the roll.

Roll the pastry over to make a long cylinder with the pastry seam underneath. Cut each cylinder into 5 cm (2 inch) rolls. Place onto baking trays lined with non-stick baking paper. Score with a sharp knife, brush with egg wash and top with poppy seeds, if using.

Bake for 15 minutes until golden brown and cooked through. Serve immediately with tomato chutney.

2 teaspoons fennel seeds
6 black peppercorns
1 pinch of freshly grated nutmeg
250 g (9 oz) lean pork, minced
½ brown onion, diced
½ carrot, finely diced
1 stalk celery, finely diced
3 sheets of frozen puff pastry
1 egg yolk, whisked with a touch of milk
poppy seeds (optional)
tomato chutney, to serve (see page 18)

I have to let you in on a secret. I have a huge vice and that is meat pies. I absolutely love them. I think it comes from when I was a kid on the Gold Coast. My mates and I would spend the whole weekend down the beach surfing, playing footy and our lunch would always be the same — meat pie and sauce, chocolate milkshake and a packet of chips — I know, I know... but things were different then. Anyway, to this day, I still hunt down a good meat pie whenever I visit a new town. Here is my recipe for a simple but great meat pie cooked with a nice drop of red!

beef and shiraz pies

MAKES 16

2 quantities of sour cream pastry
    (see recipe below)

500 g (1 lb 2 oz) chuck or round steak,
    cut into 2 cm (¾ inch) dice
2 teaspoons vegetable oil
½ brown onion, diced
½ small carrot, diced
½ stalk celery, diced
1 garlic clove, crushed
125 ml (4 fl oz/½ cup) good-quality shiraz
2 thyme sprigs, chopped
200 g (7 oz) tin chopped tomatoes
1 egg, beaten
2 teaspoons sesame seeds
tomato sauce, to serve

sour cream pastry

300 g (10½ oz/2 cups) plain
    (all-purpose) flour
125 g (4½ oz) unsalted butter, chilled
    and diced
1 free-range egg
60 g (2¼ oz/¼ cup) sour cream

Season the beef with salt and pepper. Heat the oil in a large, heavy-based casserole dish over high heat. Add half of the beef and cook for about 3–4 minutes, stirring often, until the beef is well browned all over. Remove with a slotted spoon, leaving any oil in the pan. Let the pan reheat, add the remaining beef and repeat, cooking until well browned. Set the beef aside.

Reduce the heat to low. Add the onion, carrot, celery and garlic. Cook for 2–3 minutes, until softened. Return the beef to the pan, with any juices. Add the wine and bring to the boil, deglazing the pan and stirring to combine any stuck-on bits.

Add the thyme and tomato and 125 ml (4 fl oz/½ cup) of water, season to taste. Bring to the boil then reduce the heat to a low simmer. Cook covered for about 1½ hours stirring often until the beef is tender. Transfer to a bowl and refrigerate until chilled.

For the pastry, put the flour, a pinch of salt and the butter in a food processor and pulse until combined and the mixture resembles large crumbs. Then pulse in the egg, and the sour cream. Transfer dough to a lightly floured work surface and briefly knead to bring together (do not overwork). Shape the pastry into a ball, wrap in plastic and rest in the fridge for 1 hour. Repeat to make the second quantity of pastry.

Remove the pastry from the fridge 15 minutes before using and lightly grease 16 muffin holes (125 ml (4 fl oz/½ cup capacity).

Preheat the oven to 180°C (350°F/Gas 4). Roll out the pastry on a floured work surface, or between two sheets of non-stick baking paper, to about 2–3 mm (1/16 –⅛ inch) thick. Cut out 11½ cm (4¼ inch) diameter circles to line the muffin holes and 8 cm (3¼ inch) diameter circles to use as the lids. (You may need to re-roll some of the pastry).

Spoon in the cooled meat mixture. Brush some of the beaten egg around the edges of the pastry and sit the pastry lids on top. Use a fork to gently press around the edges to seal and brush all over with the remaining egg and sprinkle with sesame seeds. Bake in the oven for 20–25 minutes, until golden. Serve with the tomato sauce.

I absolutely love Moroccan cooking – the flavours used to spice the food are phenomenal, you might think it could be too much or too confusing for the palate but when you actually taste it, you will find it's very balanced. One flavour doesn't seem to overpower another. These little 'cigars' are a lot of fun to serve at a party, firstly because they are quail (which I think is such an underrated form of protein) and also because of the cinnamon and caster sugar. It becomes a real talking point for your guests.

quail bisteeya with cinnamon and sugar

MAKES 36

Melt the butter in a large heavy-based pan and sauté the onions and quails with the spices until evenly coated. Add the chicken stock and cinnamon stick and reduce the heat to low, simmer for 15 minutes, remove the quail and cool. When cool cut the meat and skin into tiny pieces.

Strain the liquid into a clean saucepan and bring to the boil. Add the egg and stir until it is cooked and the liquid has evaporated. Return the cooked quail to the pan, add the coriander and parsley, season with salt and pepper and mix well. Set aside to cool completely.

Toast the almonds till golden. When they are cool, roughly chop and mix with the sugar and cinnamon.

Preheat the oven to 180°C (350°F/Gas 4). Lay one sheet of filo pastry on the work surface with the shortest side at the bottom. Brush with butter and fold in half by bringing the top edge to the bottom edge and brush with butter again. Then add 4 tablespoons of filling along the bottom edge of the pastry, roll it up so it resembles a thick cigar and brush the outside with more melted butter. Trim the ends and cut into 4 cm (1½ inch) cigars then place them on baking trays lined with non-stick baking paper. Repeat with remaining filo, butter and filling.

Bake for 15 minutes or until golden. To finish, sprinkle with the almond cinnamon sugar mixture and serve with the yoghurt and mint leaves.

50 g (1¾ oz) butter
½ brown onion, diced
5 deboned quails, cut in half
pinch of ground cumin
pinch of ground coriander
2 teaspoons ground cinnamon
¾ teaspoon ground ginger
⅛ teaspoon cayenne pepper
¼ teaspoon saffron threads
¼ teaspoon ground turmeric
125 ml (4 fl oz/½ cup) chicken stock
½ cinnamon stick
2 free-range eggs, lightly beaten
2 tablespoons chopped coriander
2 tablespoons chopped flat-leaf (Italian) parsley
40 g (1½ oz/¼ cup) whole blanched almonds
2 tablespoons caster (superfine) sugar
⅛ teaspoon ground cinnamon, extra
6 sheets filo pastry
100 g (3½ oz) butter, melted for brushing filo
plain yoghurt and mint leaves, to serve

This has become somewhat of a signature dish for me whenever I entertain. Whether I serve it as a finger-food or a first course, all I know is that it knocks everyone's socks off every time. It is great on its own, or with a touch of chilli oil and a bit of finely sliced basil. My favourite is to put amazing seafood in the bowl or cup, pour over the hot soup and finish with some baby herbs. The best seafood for this, in no particular order, is shaved abalone, seared scallops, steamed mussels, vongole or clams, hand-picked crabmeat, pan-roasted bug tails, fried soft shell crab or smoked trout.

sweet corn soup with mussels, basil and chilli

SERVES 20

10 corn cobs

1 onion, halved

3 garlic cloves

20 mussels, cleaned, beards removed

50 g (1¾ oz) unsalted butter

6 large French shallots, sliced

4 cloves garlic, sliced

100 ml (3½ fl oz) white wine

100 ml (3½ fl oz) pouring cream

2 teaspoons chilli oil, to serve

½ punnet baby purple basil, trimmed or
    4 basil leaves, finely shredded, to serve

Remove the kernels from the corn cobs (you should have about 1.5 kg (3 lb 5 oz) of kernels) and set aside for the soup.

Use the peeled corn cobs to make a corn stock, place them in a large pot with the onion, garlic and 4 litres (140 fl oz) of water. Bring to the boil, simmer for an hour and then remove from the heat. Allow the stock to cool for a further hour and then strain, discarding the corn cobs and reserving the corn stock to use in the soup.

To open the mussels, place them in a heated pot with a splash of water and cover with a tight-fitting lid. Cook for 2 minutes or until the mussels have opened. Remove from the heat and discard any mussels that remain closed.

Remove the mussel meat from the shells and reserve and strain any cooking liquor for the soup.

Heat the butter in a saucepan and gently cook the shallots and garlic until soft and translucent. Add the corn kernels and cook for another couple of minutes then add the wine, corn stock and cooking liquid from the mussels. Bring to the boil, reduce the heat and simmer for 20 minutes. Add the cream and cook for another 2 minutes then remove from the heat and blend until smooth. Pass through a sieve and season with salt.

Place the mussels into the bottom of small serving cups. Pour the soup over the mussels and top with the chilli oil and basil.

The grand master of Chinese cuisine and hospitality in Australia is the very affable Gilbert Lau, who 30 years ago, started what is often considered the best Chinese restaurant in Australia, The Flower Drum. He now has Lau's Family Kitchen in St Kilda. Gilbert has been a regular customer of mine at The Pantry for the last 15 years and he has kindly passed on his famous and simple scallop won ton recipe.

steamed scallop won tons

MAKES 20

Chop the prawns to a fine mince, place in a bowl with the salt, white pepper, sugar, sesame oil and potato flour and beat vigorously to a smooth, firm mixture. Add the scallop meat, Chinese broccoli, bamboo shoots and ginger and mix well. Chill the filling in the refrigerator for at least 30 minutes before wrapping.

Cut the four corners of the won ton wrapper, making 1.5 cm (⅝ inch) slits. Hold the wrapper in the palm of your left hand, place 2 teaspoons of filling in the centre of the wrapper, and wrap the sides up. The filling should be seen above the wrapper like a dim sim.

Flatten the bases slightly. Place the dumplings into a steamer basket and place over a wok of boiling water to steam for approximately 10 minutes.

Combine the light soy sauce and chilli in a bowl and serve with the won tons.

40 g (1½ oz) prawn (shrimp) meat
¼ teaspoon salt
¼ teaspoon ground white pepper
¼ teaspoon sugar
⅛ teaspoon sesame oil
1 teaspoon potato flour
200 g (7 oz) scallop meat without roe, finely diced
2 tablespoons finely diced Chinese broccoli (gai larn)
1½ tablespoons finely diced bamboo shoot
1 tablespoon finely chopped ginger
20 won ton wrappers
125 ml (4 fl oz/½ cup) light soy sauce
1 green scud chilli, thinly sliced

stand alone

SERVES 1

1 orange wedge
orange sugar (see page 242)
50 ml (½ fl oz) bourbon
10 ml (2 teaspoons) Triple Sec
30 ml (1 fl oz) lemon juice
dash of egg white
15 ml (½ fl oz) ginger and orange syrup
   (see page 239)

Use the orange wedge to run around the rim of a glass, then dip half of the rim of the glass into the orange sugar. Place the remaining ingredients in a shaker over ice, shake vigorously to emulsify the egg white and then strain into the coupette glass.

bourbon cherry sour

SERVES 1

45 ml (1½ fl oz) bourbon (Makers Mark
   works well)
15 ml (½ fl oz) maraschino liqueur
30 ml (1 fl oz) cherry puree (see page 239)
15 ml (½ fl oz) lemon juice
dash of egg white
dash of sugar syrup (see page 238)
fresh cherries with stems, to garnish

Place all the ingredients in a shaker over ice, shake vigorously to emulsify the egg white. Strain into an old fashioned glass filled with ice and garnish with cherries.

spiced blazer

SERVES 1

Pour the whisky into a stainless steel jug and then carefully light. Add the remaining ingredients and pour between another stainless steel jug four or five times, until the spices have flavoured the spirit. Pour into a cognac balloon, garnish and serve.

60 ml (2 fl oz/¼ cup) single malt whisky
    (Glenfiddich 15YO works well)
dash of sugar syrup (see page 238)
half a vanilla bean, seeds scraped
1 cinnamon stick
1 star anise
1 clove
dash of water
orange zest, star anise, cinnamon stick
    and half a vanilla bean, to garnish

lemon buttered rum

SERVES 1

Place the Port, maple syrup, lemon butter and bitters in a tumbler and mix into a paste with 15 ml (½ fl oz) of the rum. Add ice and stir to combine. Top with the remaining rum and garnish with the lemon zest.

NOTE: This recipe was inspired by Shae Silvestro, the sharpest rum shooter in Sydney.

10 ml (2 teaspoons) Port
10 ml (2 teaspoons) maple syrup
1 teaspoon good-quality lemon butter
2 dashes Angostura bitters
60 ml (2 fl oz/¼ cup) aged rum (Matusalem
    Gran Reserva 15YO works well)
lemon zest, to garnish

mulled wine

SERVES 4

Place all the ingredients in a small saucepan and leave to simmer for 15 minutes while stirring occasionally, then leave on low heat to serve to guests. Strain into a carafe, place the garnish in four wine glasses and serve.

120 ml (4 fl oz) Cognac

60 ml (2 fl oz/¼ cup) Grand Marnier

300 ml (10½ fl oz) cabernet merlot

120 ml (4 fl oz) mandarin juice

8 blood orange wedges

6 plum slices

1 cinnamon stick

2 cloves

1 star anise

1 whole nutmeg

4 large orange zests studded with a clove
    and 4 slices of plum with cinnamon
    sugar (see page 242), to garnish

spiced apple toddy

SERVES 1

Place the whisky, cinnamon, clove and star anise in a stainless steel cup or jug. Add 10–15 ml (½ fl oz) boiling hot water. Stir in the Pomme Verte, apple juice, lemon juice and twist leave to sit for 2 minutes then pour or strain into an old fashioned glass. Garnish with the cinnamon stick and apple crisp to serve.

45 ml (1½ fl oz) single malt whisky
    (Glenfiddich 12YO works well)

1 cinnamon stick

1 clove

1 star anise

15 ml (½ fl oz) Pomme Verte (clear green
    apple liqueur)

30 ml (1 fl oz) cloudy apple juice

5 ml (1 teaspoon) lemon juice

lemon twist

cinnamon stick with apple crisp, to garnish
    (see page 241)

spiced pear sour

SERVES 1

45 ml (1½ fl oz) single malt whisky
    (Glenfiddich 12YO works well)
15 ml (½ fl oz) spiced syrup
    (see page 239)
30 ml (1 fl oz) pear purée (see page 239)
15 ml (½ fl oz) lemon juice
dash of egg white
cinnamon sugar (see page 242), to garnish

Place all the ingredients in a shaker and shake vigorously to emulsify the egg white. Strain and serve straight up in a champagne flute. Sprinkle with the cinnamon sugar to serve.

billy ray toddy

SERVES 1

45 ml (1½ fl oz) bourbon (Makers
    Mark works well)
1 cinnamon stick
1 clove
1 star anise
15 ml (½ fl oz) white crème de cacao
    (white chocolate liqueur)
5 ml (1 teaspoon) lemon juice
orange twist
cinnamon stick, to garnish

Place the bourbon, cinnamon, clove and star anise in a stainless steel cup or jug with 15 ml (½ fl oz) boiling hot water, then add the crème de cacao, lemon juice and orange twist. Leave to sit for 1 minute then strain, pour into a small collins glass and garnish with the cinnamon stick.

NOTE: The recipe was inspired by 'Billy Ray Bourbon' AKA Jared Plummer.

black tie

Black tie means it's time to pull out the best cutlery and crockery, polish up those glasses and throw away the paper napkins. As for the drinks, it's everything to do with signature touches; the tailored ice, rare-release spirits and unique ingredients – there's something for the entertaining king, queen, prince or princess in this section.

Teague Ezard's eponymous restaurant in Melbourne has always been a standout for me — he is a chef who has a great take on flavours as well as presentation. It was while filming with him a few years ago that he taught me this amazing concoction. I was truly blown away, not just because of the wasabi in the mix (you can play with that to see how much kick you want) but also by how elegant and simple the recipe actually was. This is why I have to feature it in this book — it really is a killer way to serve oysters!

japanese-inspired oyster shooter with sake, mirin and wasabi

MAKES 20

shooter mix
500 ml (17 fl oz/2 cups) mirin
125 ml (4 fl oz/½ cup) sake
35 ml (1 fl oz) rice vinegar
1 tablespoon light soy sauce
1 tablespoon wasabi powder

20 freshly shucked oysters

Place the mirin and sake in a small saucepan over a high heat and burn off the alcohol, when ready remove from the heat and set aside to cool. Once cool, strain, add the rice vinegar and taste for a balance of sweet and sour. Add the light soy sauce for colour and flavour, then add the wasabi powder, mixing well to combine. Refrigerate until the wasabi powder has fallen to the bottom and you are left with a clear liquid.

Strain the liquid into a jug making sure not to disturb the impurities at the bottom and refrigerate until needed.

Serve in shot glasses, first placing an oyster in each glass and then pouring over some of the shooter mix.

This is such a simple recipe to prepare and very rewarding as your guests will think you have been slaving all day to create it. Make sure you use beautiful, freshly cooked crabmeat (you can buy crabmeat already cooked and ready to go from the fish markets). Mud, spanner, blue swimmer, sand, snow or king crab are perfect to use but I think mud crab is my favourite for this recipe.

mud crab tortellini 'aglio e olio'

MAKES 20

Mix the crabmeat, parsley, lemon zest and oil together and season with salt and cracked black pepper.

Place a small amount of filling in the centre of each gow gee wrapper, then use your finger to dab a small amount of water on the rim of the circle. Fold over into a half-moon shape and seal. Take the 2 corner points and twist around your fingers to shape the tortellini.

For the sauce, heat the oil with the garlic, chilli and anchovy and cook until just starting to change colour. Add the parsley and cook for 10 seconds to release the flavour. Add the anchovy oil and season with sea salt. Cook the tortellini in boiling, salted water until tender and then lift out with a slotted spoon. Toss the pasta in the aglio e olio sauce and serve immediately either on a Chinese spoon or small plates. Garnish with lemon zest, grated bottarga and parsley.

20 gow gee wrappers

filling
150 g (5½ oz) cooked and picked
   mud crab
1 tablespoon chopped parsley
2 teaspoons grated lemon zest
3 teaspoons olive oil

sauce
100 ml (3½ fl oz) extra virgin olive oil
3 garlic cloves, finely chopped
1 long red chilli, finely chopped
2 anchovies, chopped
1 teaspoon chopped flat-leaf
   (Italian) parsley
dash of anchovy oil

1 tablespoon grated lemon zest
1 tablespoon grated bottarga (optional)
chopped parsley, to serve

Nothing says opulence more than caviar, but you have to be careful what you serve it with, as you don't want the caviar flavour to disappear. I think the best way to serve it is with crème fraîche and a just-cooked blini (buckwheat pancake) so it is still warm. The next best thing to bulk it up is to team the caviar with some smoked salmon — you'll still feel like you get a caviar hit and the smoked salmon and crème fraîche work so well together. Other nice accompaniments for your caviar are finely chopped cornichons, red onion, chives, dill, boiled egg … mmmm, I'm getting hungry!

smoked salmon blini with crème fraîche and caviar

MAKES 20

1 teaspoon active dry yeast
110 g (3¾ oz) plain (all-purpose) flour
90 g (3¼ oz/⅗ cup) buckwheat flour
1 free-range egg, separated
40 g (1½ oz) unsalted butter, melted
½ teaspoon sugar
185 ml (6 fl oz/¾ cup) lukewarm milk
½ teaspoon sea salt
200 g (7 oz) crème fraîche
10 good quality smoked salmon slices,
    cut into pieces
100 g (3½ oz) avruga caviar
20 small dill sprigs

Combine the yeast and 190 ml (6½ fl oz) of lukewarm water in a large bowl, stir to dissolve, then stand in a warm place for 10 minutes or until foamy. Slowly whisk in the plain flour, then cover with a clean tea towel (dish towel) and stand in a warm place for 1 hour or until doubled in size.

In a separate bowl, combine the buckwheat flour, egg yolk, 1½ tablespoons of the melted butter, sugar, milk and sea salt and whisk to combine, and then gently fold into the yeast mixture. Cover and stand in a warm place for 1 hour or until risen by half.

Whisk the egg whites until soft peaks form and fold through the batter. Heat a heavy-based non-stick frying pan over medium heat, brush with the remaining butter and cook tablespoonfuls of batter, in batches, for 1–2 minutes or until bubbles appear, then turn and cook for another minute or until cooked through. Keep warm.

To assemble, spread the blini with the crème fraîche and arrange swirls of smoked salmon on top. Finish with a further dollop of crème fraîche, spoon some caviar on top and garnish with the dill.

This recipe was given to me by a very good friend and one of the most exciting chefs in Australia – Raita Noda. I met him about 10 years ago when I was recommended Rise, his first restaurant. His interpretation of modern Japanese was brilliant and delicious. A true artist in every sense of the word and even better than that was his love of seafood. This is one of the highlights from his menu.

soft shell crab taco

MAKES 20

To make the marinated salmon roe, soak the roe in water for 1 hour to reduce the salt content and the strong fish flavour. Place the sake and mirin in a saucepan and bring to the boil to allow the alcohol to evaporate, set aside to cool. Combine the salmon roe, sake and mirin mixture and the light soy sauce in a bowl and place it in the refrigerate overnight. To serve, drain the salmon roe and discard the liquid.

To make the marinated bean sprouts, cook them in boiling water for about 10 seconds with a pinch of salt. Drain well and cool. Toss with remaining ingredients and refrigerate until needed. Drain to serve.

To make the cajun spice mix, combine all the spices.

Heat the oil in a wok or deep saucepan to 170°C (325°F). Fry the gow gee wrappers briefly until crisp and golden and drain on kitchen paper. Lightly dust the soft shell crab with the potato starch, shake off any excess. Deep-fry for 2–3 minutes or until golden brown and crisp. Drain on kitchen paper and dust with the cajun mix.

To serve, place some marinated bean sprouts and soft shell crab on 20 of the crispy gow gee wrappers. Top with some leek, cucumber and a dollop of mayonnaise, and finish with ¼ teaspoon of the marinated salmon roe. Place the remaining crispy gow gee wrapper halves on top.

vegetable oil, for deep-frying
20 gow gee wrappers, cut in half
10 soft shell crabs (about 100 g each (3½ oz), cut in two pieces (remove the mustard part of the crab when cutting in half)
100 g (3½ oz) potato starch
¼ leek, white part only, finely shredded
1 cucumber, seeds removed, finely shredded
4 tablespoons whole-egg mayonnaise

marinated salmon roe
65 g (2¼ oz) salmon roe
2½ tablespoons cooking sake
2 tablespoons mirin
2 tablespoons light soy sauce

marinated bean sprouts
180 g (6 oz/2 cups) bean sprouts
100 ml (3½ fl oz) light soy sauce
120 ml (4 fl oz) mirin
1 teaspoon sesame oil
1 teaspoon white sesame seeds
pinch of ichimi Japanese chilli power (available from Asian supermarkets)

cajun spice mix
2 tablespoons chilli powder
4 teaspoons paprika
1 teaspoon each of cayenne pepper, garlic, onion powder, ground cumin, curry powder, cracked black pepper
3 teaspoons salt

Once a year I travel to New York to see what's happening with the food and bar scene. On my last visit I happened to dine at the most exciting restaurant I have eaten in for years, Marea. The owner/chef Michael White came and joined me for an hour. We discussed his philosophy on Italian food and the dishes I was about to enjoy. What an amazing experience, not only for my tastebuds but also my heart, as I listened to another chef talk so honestly and passionately about the food he produces. This morsel was the highlight of my evening and I have attempted to re-create it as best as my memory allows. If you can't find lardo, just a drizzle of extra virgin olive oil will be fine, and of course only the freshest sea urchin should be used.

fresh sea urchin on crouton with lardo

MAKES 20

1 day-old sourdough baguette
extra virgin olive oil
40 sea urchin roe (or roe from 8 live sea
   urchins) (see note)
20 thin 5 cm (2 inch) long slices lardo
   (see note)
lemon wedges, to serve

Preheat the oven to 160°C (315°F/Gas 2–3). To make the croutons slice the baguette into 5 mm (¼ inch) thick slices and lay on a baking tray. Drizzle with extra virgin olive oil, season with sea salt and cook for 5 minutes or until golden brown. Increase oven temperature to 170°C (325°F/Gas 3).

Lay the sea urchin on the toasted croutons and sprinkle with sea salt.

Place the lardo on top and return to the oven for 2–3 minutes to melt the fat and warm the sea urchin. Drizzle with extra virgin olive oil and serve immediately with lemon wedges.

NOTE: Sea urchin roe is available from specialist seafood suppliers. If using fresh sea urchin remove the five fingers of roe from the spiny shell. Lardo is pork back fat cured with herbs, available from select Italian butchers.

This is a dish I learned from Shannon Bennett, a good mate of mine. About seven years ago Shannon came and did a dinner with me at my restaurant for his first book launch. This is one of the canapés he prepared on the night and as often happens when chefs work together, they get inspired to go and try new things. That said, this dish didn't need any tinkering — it was perfect and I have served it to tens of thousands of guests over the years. It's always a winner.

steak tartare with quail egg and black sea salt

MAKES 24

Preheat the oven to 160°C (315°F/Gas 2–3). To make the croutons slice the baguette into twenty 1 cm (½ inch) thick slices, cut out rounds using a 4 cm (1½ inch) diameter cutter and lay on a baking tray. Drizzle with some olive oil and salt and cook for 5–10 minutes or until golden brown.

Chop the meat very finely with a sharp, clean knife and chopping board.

Mix the mustard and anchovy in a large stainless steel bowl. Add the tomato sauce, Worcestershire sauce, Tabasco, and some pepper and mix well. Slowly whisk in the oil, and then the cognac, if using. Fold in the shallots, capers, cornichons, parsley and a little sea salt.

Add the meat to the bowl and mix well with a spoon or your hands. Divide the mix into 24 portions and using a 3 cm (1¼ inch) diameter cutter as a mould, form the meat into discs on the croutons.

In batches, using a cold non-stick frying pan, crack open the quail eggs and slowly cook them over a medium heat. Just cook the eggs until the egg white is white. Then allow to cool while still in the pan. Remove from the pan. Using a 3 cm (1¼ inch) diameter round cutter carefully cut out the quail eggs, ensuring that you have the white part and the egg yolk so it looks like a mini fried egg. Once you have finished cutting out the eggs, place an egg on top of each tartare crouton and finish with a touch of black salt.

1 day-old sourdough baguette
olive oil
200 g (7 oz) beef eye fillet
1 tablespoon dijon mustard
2 anchovy fillets, finely chopped
   (Ortiz brand works well)
1 tablespoon tomato sauce (ketchup)
2 teaspoons Worcestershire sauce
Tabasco sauce, to taste
cracked black pepper
1½ tablespoons extra virgin olive oil
1½ teaspoons Cognac (optional)
2 tablespoons finely chopped
   French shallot (eschalot)
30 g (1 oz) capers, rinsed
30 g (1 oz) cornichons, finely chopped
small handful flat-leaf (Italian) parsley,
   finely chopped
20 quail eggs
pinch black sea salt

Luxury and indulgence, culinarily speaking, for me is jamón Ibérico, caviar, toro (fatty tuna belly), Roquefort and of course, foie gras. I still recall the first time I tried all of these delicacies ... jamón was in Barcelona, Spain, caviar at Neil Perry's Rockpool restaurant, toro in Tokyo, Roquefort in France and foie gras at Thomas Keller's French Laundry in the Napa Valley. I wouldn't be able to choose one over the other but nor would I want to eat them every day either — they are a luxury item and because of that they should only be eaten or served on special occasions. This recipe is one I've been serving at high-end parties for years and one I always get excited about when serving. Enjoy the flavours!

foie gras pâté on toasted brioche with sauternes jelly

MAKES 40

25 g (1 oz) butter, for frying livers (see note)

250 g (9 oz) duck livers (soaked in 100 ml (3½ fl oz) milk for 2 hours, then strained)

1 large garlic clove, finely chopped

1 French shallot (eschalot), finely chopped

2 teaspoons chopped thyme

30 ml (1 fl oz) brandy

30 ml (1 fl oz) port

30 ml (1 fl oz) Madeira

1 tablespoon dijon mustard

50 g (1¾ oz) foie gras

165 g (5¾ oz) butter, at room temperature

1 free-range egg yolk

½ brioche loaf, sliced into 20 small squares

finely shredded purple basil or baby herbs, to serve

sauternes jelly

100 ml (3½ fl oz) sauternes or other sweet dessert wine

2 x 2 g gold gelatine leaves

To make the sauternes jelly, place the sauterne in a small saucepan and bring to a simmer. Meanwhile soak the gelatine leaves in cold water until softened. Squeeze the gelatine leaves to remove any excess water and whisk into the sauternes to dissolve. Strain into a shallow container and refrigerate for 1 hour or until set.

Melt some of the butter in a frying pan over medium heat and fry the liver in batches until just rare, wiping out the pan between batches. Remove from the pan.

Add the garlic, shallot and thyme to the pan and sauté until translucent, then add the alcohol and flame to reduce to a honey consistency. Transfer to a blender, add the livers, mustard and foie gras and purée until smooth. Add the butter gradually and season with salt and pepper. Add the egg yolk and blend until smooth, then pass through a sieve to get it extra smooth.

Press into ramekins or a small terrine mould lined with plastic wrap, cover and leave to set in the refrigerator for 4 hours or overnight.

Preheat the oven to 160°C (315°F/Gas 2–3), place the brioche squares on a baking tray. Cook for 2 minutes or until golden. Spread the pâté onto the toasted brioche, cut the jelly into small cubes and place on the top pâté with purple basil.

NOTE: To make clarified butter, melt cold, cubed butter until the fat separates from the milky solids. Stand, skim surface then pour off the clear (clarified) butter. Note that 250 g (9 oz) butter will give you 200 ml (7 fl oz) clarified butter. Clarified butter or ghee is available from supermarkets.

I go fishing in the Northern Territory every year and each time I pop into my favourite restaurant in Darwin, Hanuman. It's owned by Jimmy Shu and offers a mix of Malay, Indian and Thai cuisines. One dish I always order is the Hanuman oysters. They are cooked with a mix of lemongrass, lime juice, fish sauce and palm sugar along with a few other aromatics and although I am an oyster purist and love them just freshly shucked, this recipe easily does them more than justice.

hanuman's signature oysters with lemongrass, sweet basil, chilli and fresh coriander

MAKES 20

Cut roots and 5 cm (2 inches) of the stems from the coriander and chop finely, reserving the leaves. Finely chop the basil stems. Process the roots and stems, galangal, lemongrass, chilli, garlic, lime juice, fish sauce and palm sugar in a food processor until finely chopped. Check for the balance of sweet, sour, salty and hot and adjust if necessary.

Preheat the oven to 200°C (400°F/Gas 6). Place the oysters on a baking tray lined with rock salt and cook for 1 minute or until warm (you could do this under a hot grill (broiler) if you like). Drizzle each oyster with a teaspoon of sauce, scatter with the basil and coriander leaves and serve with the remaining sauce on the side.

2 coriander stalks, roots attached

1 sweet basil stalk, leaves removed and stems reserved

½ teaspoon finely grated galangal

2 tablespoons thinly sliced lemongrass, white part only

1 small red chilli, finely chopped

1 garlic clove, finely chopped

60 ml (2 fl oz/¼ cup) lime juice

30 ml (1 fl oz) fish sauce

2 tablespoons grated palm sugar (jaggery)

20 Pacific oysters, freshly shucked in the shell

rock salt

floral foam

SERVES 1

1 lime zest
45 ml (1½ fl oz) vodka (Zubrowka Bison
    Grass vodka works well)
15 ml (½ fl oz) Pomme Verte (clear green
    apple liqueur)
5 ml (1 teaspoon) lime juice
30 ml (1 fl oz) clear apple juice
elderflower foam (see page 245)

Stain the glass with the lime zest. Place all the ingredients, except the foam, in the shaker over ice, shake and then strain into the glass and top with the foam.

enviously green

SERVES 1

essence of Jasmine green tea
    (see page 244)
50 ml (1½ fl oz) Beefeater 24 Gin
10 ml (2 teaspoons) Pomme Verte
    (clear green apple liqueur)
5 ml (1 teaspoon) Cinzano Bianco
5 ml (1 teaspoon) elderflower cordial
zest of 1 lime
garden flower, to garnish

Place the essence of jasmine green tea in a fine mist spray bottle and spray a martini glass with a fine mist. Staining the glass with the tea allows the tea's floral notes to enhance the elderflower and tea notes in the Beefeater 24 Gin. Place all the remaining ingredients in a martini pitcher with ice, stir and then strain into the glass with a julep strainer and garnish with the garden flower petal.

luxury side car

SERVES 1

Use the orange wedge to run around the rim of a martini glass, then dip half of the rim of the glass into the orange sugar. Place all ingredients in a shaker over ice and shake. Strain into the glass and garnish with skewered sultanas and raisins.

1 orange wedge
orange sugar (see page 242)
45 ml (1½ fl oz) Hennessy XO Cognac
15 ml (½ fl oz) Grand Marnier Centenaire
30 ml (1 fl oz) lemon juice
dash of sugar syrup (see pg 238)
dash of orange bitters (Regan's works well)
skewered sultanas (golden raisins) and
**   raisins, to garnish**

luxury french '75'

SERVES 1

Stain a champagne glass with the orange bitters. Add the Cognac, lemon juice and sugar syrup to the glass and stir before topping with the Champagne. Garnish with the candied orange.

dash of orange bitters
30 ml (1 fl oz) Hennessy XO Cognac
5 ml (1 teaspoon) lemon juice
dash of sugar syrup (see page 238)
topped with Champagne (Perrier Jouet
**   Belle Époque works well)**
half a candied orange slice, to garnish
**   (see page 209)**

the ron 23

SERVES 1

dash of orange bitters (Regan's works well)
50 ml (1½ fl oz) Ron Zacapa Rum Centenario
    23 Anos
10 ml (2 teaspoons) Hennessy
    Cognac VSOP
10 ml (2 teaspoons) Lillet Blanc
5 ml (1 teaspoon) white crème de cacao
    (white chocolate liqueur)
5 ml (1 teaspoon) Cointreau
dark chocolate webbing, to garnish
    (see note)

Stain the glass with the orange bitters and then place all the ingredients in a martini pitcher over ice. Stir and strain using a julep strainer into an old fashioned glass over cracked ice and garnish with a dark chocolate web. This is a drink to cherish, reflect on the world and toast well being. This spirit has been rated by the Beverage Tasting Institute 98 out of 100.

NOTE: For the chocolate webbing, melt 100 g (3½ oz) dark chocolate (70% cocoa) in a bowl over a saucepan of simmering water. Spoon into a small piping (icing) bag and pipe into webbed shapes on a baking tray lined with non-stick baking paper. Refrigerate to set.

sauternes spritzer

SERVES 1

1 lemon zest
75 ml (2¼ fl oz) pinot gris
15 ml (½ fl oz) lemon myrtle liqueur
25 ml (1¾ fl oz) sparkling mineral water
sauterne jelly piece (see page 195)

Run the lemon zest around a wine goblet to stain with lemon essence and discard, then add the pinot gris, lemon myrtle liqueur and mineral water and stir. Serve with a sauternes jelly piece to enhance the wine.

signature chivas 18

SERVES 1

Place the ice sphere in an old fashioned glass. Add the remaining ingredients, the ice and stir before garnishing with the dark chocolate web.

1 ice sphere (see page 246)
50 ml (1½ fl oz) Chivas Regal 18YO
10 ml (2 teaspoons) spiced apricot and
    vanilla syrup (see page 239)
5 ml (1 teaspoon) white crème de cacao
    (white chocolate liqueur)
dark chocolate webbing, to garnish
    (see page 202)

solera mistress

SERVES 1

Use the orange wedge to run around the rim of a glass, then dip half of the rim of the glass into the orange sugar. Place all the ingredients into the glass over the vanilla ice sphere. Garnish with the split vanilla bean.

1 orange wedge
orange sugar (see page 242)
1 vanilla ice sphere (see page 246)
45 ml (1½ fl oz) rum (Glen Fiddich 15YO
    rum works well)
15 ml (½ fl oz) Amontillado Sherry
5 ml (1 teaspoon) Cointreau
dash of orange bitters
half a split vanilla bean, to garnish

high tea

Desserts and cocktails can sometimes be one and the same. They share common ingredients such as chocolate, coffee and flavoured liqueurs. And the perfect end to any party has to be an espresso chilli martini with a rich tiramisù.

To finish off a party you need to have something elegant and light and these fit the bill perfectly. You can pre-make the cones up to a day before and keep them in an airtight container, you can also pre-make the filling. If the cones are too hard or time-consuming just cook up little rounds of the filo pastry instead and pipe the mixture on top — I find pistachios are the perfect accompaniment to these.

cannoli with pistachio

MAKES 20

8 sheets of filo pastry
100 g (3½ oz) butter, melted
50 g (1¾ oz) pure icing (confectioners') sugar, sifted
45 g (1½ oz) pistachios, finely sliced
extra pure icing (confectioners') sugar, for dusting

candied citrus rind
4 oranges (navel oranges are best) or 6 lemons
440 g (15½ oz/2 cups) sugar

filling
300 g (10½ oz) ricotta
50 g (1¾ oz) candied orange rind, finely chopped
50 g (1¾ oz) candied lemon rind, finely chopped
75 g (2½ oz) pure icing (confectioners') sugar, sifted
20 ml (½ fl oz) limoncello

To make the candied citrus rind, wash the fruit well and dry. Remove the peel from the fruit using a sharp knife — cutting to ensure you are removing the skin and pith in long pieces and leaving behind the fruit. (To make both the orange and lemon versions of this recipe they should be blanched and cooked separately.) Bring a saucepan of water to the boil and blanch the orange or lemon rind for a few seconds, then strain under cold running water. Repeat this process twice. Place 500 ml (17 fl oz/2 cups) of water and the sugar in a small saucepan over high heat. Bring to the boil, stirring to dissolve the sugar. Then add the orange or lemon rind, reduce the heat and gently simmer for 30 minutes or until translucent. Allow to cool in the saucepan. This recipe will make 150 g (5½ oz) candied orange rind or 100 g (3½ oz) candied lemon rind.

Preheat the oven to 180°C (350°F/Gas 4). Lay out one filo sheet, brush with some melted butter and dust with some icing sugar, top with another sheet and brush with some more butter. Cut the layered sheet into rounds using an 8 cm (3¼ inch) round cutter. You should get 5 rounds. Repeat the process with the remaining filo sheets. Shape the filo pastry into cones, using twenty 8 cm (3¼ inch) long cream horn moulds, wrapping the pastry around the moulds.

Place the pastry cones on baking trays lined with non-stick baking paper and bake for 3–4 minutes, until crisp and golden. Set aside to cool slightly, then remove the mould. Cool completely. For the filling, combine the ricotta, candied citrus rind, sugar and limoncello and mix well. Pipe into the cones, sprinkle with the pistachios and dust with icing sugar to serve.

This is the ultimate dessert recipe – chocolate, sugar, butter, flour and eggs – very hard to mess up and looks amazing when you serve it to finish off the meal at a party. Serve the fondant in cups, glasses or some great crockery with ice cream, double cream, whipped cream, berries or cherries to finish it off. Just make sure you don't serve it straight from the oven as there's nothing worse than burning your friend's and family's mouths.

chocolate fondant

MAKES 22

210 g (7½ oz) dark chocolate (70% cocoa)
135 g (4¾ oz) butter, chopped
6 free-range eggs
210 g (7½ oz) caster (superfine) sugar
105 g (3½ oz) plain (all-purpose) flour, sifted
cocoa powder, for dusting

Preheat the oven to 180°C (350°F/Gas 4). Grease 22 small 5 cm (2 inch) diameter ramekins (dariole moulds) or 50 ml (1¾ fl oz) capacity small cups and place on baking trays.

Break the chocolate into small pieces and melt it with the butter in a bowl set over a saucepan of gently simmering water. Remove from the heat.

Beat the eggs with the sugar for 6–8 minutes or until tripled in volume, then gently fold through the flour.

Gradually fold in the melted chocolate and butter. Pour into the ramekins but do not fill to the top. Leave at least a 1 cm (½ inch) gap from the rim of the ramekin to allow it to rise during the cooking process.

Bake for 5–6 minutes until firm to the touch. When the fondant is ready the outer part should be firm like a chocolate muffin and the inner part, liquid. Allow to stand for 2 minutes before serving, dusted with cocoa powder.

Serve the fondants hot on their own or with custard, whipped cream, ice cream or berries.

I've been making and serving this dish to finish off a meal for years — I never tire of making, serving or eating it. I think it could be the easiest recipe I've ever made and a stunning way to end a meal in order to enliven and clean the palate.

grapefruit and campari granita

SERVES 20

600 ml (21 fl oz) ruby red grapefruit juice
200 ml (7 fl oz) sugar syrup, chilled
   (see page 238)
Campari (or any alcohol such as vodka
   or gin), to taste
10 pink grapefruit segments, cut into
   small dice

Mix the juice and sugar syrup together, then add the alcohol to taste. Pour into a shallow tray and freeze for a few hours. Run a fork through the frozen mixture to rough it up into ice shavings. Repeat the process again of firming up and breaking up.

   Spoon the grapefruit into glasses, top with the granita and pour over more alcohol if desired.

An old mate of mine, Alex Zabotto-Bentley has kindly passed on his mother Anita's recipe for Krapfen (which translated means doughnut). Anita takes a few days before Christmas to prepare all the goodies. From krapfen to crostoli Triestini, strudelto, frittolle, they are all amazing and made with so much Italian love. Krapfen takes a while to create so make sure you have lots of family members around to enjoy them. You have to be dedicated as there is lots of down time while you wait for the dough to rise. But stick with it, the more it rises, the lighter and fluffier the doughnuts are.

anita's doughnut recipe

MAKES 40

Combine 60 ml (2 fl oz/¼ cup) lukewarm water in a bowl with the yeast and set aside for 30 minutes.

Place the flour, sugar, salt and lemon zest in the bowl of an electric mixer, fitted with a dough hook. Pour in the yeast and water, add the milk, egg yolks, rum and butter and mix until combined. Mix for 4–5 minutes or until the dough is elastic.

Place the dough in a greased bowl, cover with a tea towel (dish towel) and leave in a warm place until doubled in size (about 1½–2 hours).

Punch the dough, and then knead and roll it to form a long sausage (about 25 cm/10 inches long) on lightly floured surface. Cover again for 30 minutes.

Roll the dough into a sausage again so it is about 40 cm (16 inches) long and cut off 1 cm (½ inch) sections. Roll into balls on a clean surface and place on a floured surface again. Let rise for another 15 minutes.

Heat the vegetable oil in a large deep saucepan to 180°C (350°F). Deep-fry in batches for 2 minutes each side until golden brown. Drain on kitchen paper, then immediately roll in the sugar to coat.

Place the jam in a small piping (icing) bag and while the doughnuts are still warm, make a small hole in the side and pipe in the jam until the doughnuts feel dense.

Mmmm, apricot-doughnuty goodness. Serve immediately with coffee.

2 teaspoons active dried yeast
450 g (1 lb/3 cups) plain (all-purpose) flour, unsifted
55 g (2 oz/¼ cup) sugar
1½ teaspoons salt
finely grated zest of 1 lemon
250 ml (9 fl oz) milk
2 free-range egg yolks, beaten
1 tablespoon white rum
60 g (2¼ oz) butter, at room temperature
vegetable oil, for deep frying
extra sugar, to coat
315 g (11¼ oz/1 cup) good-quality apricot jam

Who can say 'no' to a lemon meringue tart — they're always a hit at a party. If you want, you can make and fill them with the lemon curd but for something truly memorable, make the Italian meringue and using a blow torch or grill, brown the tops of the tarts.

lemon tarts with lavender

MAKES 20

Dry out the lavender buds in a very low heat oven, 70°C (150°F/Gas ¼), on a baking tray for approximately 3 hours. When dry, blend the buds in a food processor until finely chopped.

To make the lemon curd, whisk the whole eggs, yolks and sugar in a small saucepan to combine. Place the saucepan over low heat, add the butter, lemon zest and juice and whisk continuously until thickened. Strain through a sieve, cover with plastic wrap on the surface and cool completely.

To make the pastry, cream the butter and sugar together using an electric mixer, add a pinch of salt and mix. Add the egg yolks and mix to combine. Scrape down the sides, add the flour and mix slowly until just combined. Form into a disc and wrap in plastic wrap. Refrigerate for 30 minutes. Grease 20 mini-muffin tin holes or small tartlet moulds with some butter. Roll out the pastry between sheets of non-stick baking paper to 2–3 mm (¹⁄₁₆–⅛ inch) thick. Cut out circles with a 6½ cm (2½ inch) diameter round cutter and line the muffin holes, pushing the pastry gently into the bases.

Rest in the refrigerator for 10 minutes. Preheat the oven to 180°C (350°F/Gas 4). Line the pastry with non-stick baking paper and fill with rice (or baking beans) and bake for about 8 minutes or until starting to go golden around the edges. Take out of the oven and remove the paper and rice. Brush the tarts with the egg and return to the oven for 2 minutes or until golden (this helps to seal any cracks and to give it a hard glaze so that the tart filling doesn't seep through the pastry). When golden, remove and cool.

Place the sugar into a saucepan over high heat and just cover it with water. Stir to dissolve the sugar and brush the sides down with cold water, using a pastry brush to stop the sugar syrup from crystallising. Bring to the boil and then checking with a candy thermometer, take the temperature to 121°C (235°F).

Meanwhile, whisk the egg whites using an electric mixer with a whisk attachment until they begin to fluff up. Pour in the hot sugar syrup gradually in a steady stream. The mixture will become velvety and bright white. Beat for about 5 minutes or until the mixture has cooled.

Pipe the curd into the tart cases to half full. Then pipe or spoon some of the meringue on top. Use a blow torch to flame the top if you like.

Sprinkle the tarts with the lavender and serve.

20 mini sweet shortcrust tart shells (see recipe below)

½ bunch lavender, buds removed
150 g (5½ oz) caster (superfine) sugar
75 ml (2¼ fl oz) free-range egg whites

lemon curd

2 free-range eggs
2 free-range egg yolks
165 g (5¾ oz/¾ cup) caster (superfine) sugar
80 g (2¾ oz) chilled unsalted butter, chopped
zest and juice of 2 lemons (about ½ cup of juice)

sweet shortcrust pastry

200 g (7 oz) unsalted butter, softened
100 g (3½ oz) pure icing (confectioners') sugar, sifted
2 free-range egg yolks
250 g (9 oz/1⅔ cup) plain (all-purpose) flour, sifted
1 free-range egg, beaten

I can remember when I first opened The Pantry in Brighton some 18 years ago, I had cake and cookie jars on display. One of my all-time favourite jobs was making the cakes and cookies which is funny because I've never really enjoyed eating them (I don't have a sweet tooth at all) but I really enjoyed the technical aspects of baking. This is a simple recipe to try out your baking skills and the end result is magnificent.

strawberry shortcake

MAKES 20

50 g (1¾ oz) strawberry jam
6 strawberries
pure icing (confectioners') sugar,
   sifted, for dusting

yoghurt mix

250 g (9 oz/1 cup) plain yoghurt
150 g (5½ oz) pure icing (confectioners')
   sugar, sifted
2 vanilla beans, split and scraped

vanilla sponge

180 ml (6 fl oz) free-range egg whites
125 g (4½ oz) caster (superfine) sugar
100 ml (3½ fl oz) free-range egg yolks
60 g (2¼ oz) plain (all-purpose) flour
60 g (2¼ oz/½ cup) cornflour (cornstarch)
¼ teaspoon vanilla extract

To make the yoghurt mix, combine the yoghurt, icing sugar and vanilla seeds in a bowl. Place in a sieve lined with muslin (cheesecloth) over a deep bowl to drain overnight. This should allow the excess liquid to strain out leaving the mix a nice creamy consistency.

Preheat the oven to 160°C (315°F/Gas 2–3). To make the vanilla sponge, beat the egg whites with the sugar for approximately 5 minutes to firm peaks, add the yolks and beat until thick enough to hold a trail. Gently sift over the flour and cornflour, add the vanilla and fold through gently.

Grease two flat 30 cm (12 inch) baking trays and line with non-stick baking paper.

Spread half of the amount of sponge mix on to each tray and spread the mix out evenly to 1 cm (½ inch) thick. Bake for 5 minutes or until light golden and cooked through. Set aside to cool.

Using a 4 cm (1½ inch) diameter round cutter, cut 40 discs from the sponge. Spread a small amount of jam on half of the discs. Slice the strawberries and lay 2 slices of strawberry on top of the jam. Pipe or spoon some of the yoghurt mix on top then cover with the remaining sponge discs. Dust with the icing sugar and serve these gorgeous treats on a platter.

There are classic desserts that have stood the test of time and I think the Italian tiramisù would be in my top five. There are so many different methods for making it but the main ingredients are Marsala, coffee, sponge finger biscuits and mascarpone. This looks so nice when presented in a glass or small crockery dish sprinkled with chocolate and is a great way to end a night of wonderful food.

mini tiramisù

MAKES 20

Beat the mascarpone in a mixing bowl until soft peaks form. In a separate bowl beat the eggs and caster sugar until soft peaks form, then fold in the mascarpone. Set aside.

Combine the coffee and Marsala in a shallow bowl. Dip the savoiardi biscuit pieces, one at a time, quickly into the coffee mixture. Spoon some of the mascarpone mix in a small glass then top with some pieces of biscuit then top with mascarpone mix.

Dust with the cocoa and top with the cocoa nibs or grated chocolate shavings and serve.

250 g (9 oz) mascarpone

2 free-range eggs

50 g (1¾ oz) caster (superfine) sugar

150 ml (5 fl oz) freshly brewed strong coffee, cooled

2 tablespoons Marsala

10 savoiardi biscuits, broken into pieces

cocoa powder, for dusting

40 g (1½ oz) raw cocoa nibs (available from specialty food stores) soaked in sugar syrup (see page 238), or chocolate shavings

If you're like me and not a huge fan of overly sweet desserts but prefer something light, then this is the answer for you. You can basically use any type of sorbet/gelato/ice cream or granita for this along with whatever fresh fruit is in season or even stewed fruit in autumn or winter. The possibilities are endless. It's so easy to make for a large group of people and it looks very impressive.

yoghurt gelato with summer berries

MAKES 20

yoghurt gelato

620 g (1 lb 6 oz) plain yoghurt
200 g (7 oz) caster (superfine) sugar
125 ml (4 fl oz/½ cup) cream

berry compote

100 g (3½ oz) sugar
thick orange zest
100 g (3½ oz) raspberries
100 g (3½ oz) blueberries
100 g (3½ oz) strawberries
   cut into quarters
20 mint leaves, to serve

To make the yoghurt gelato, mix all the ingredients together in a bowl and let it sit for 5 minutes, so the caster sugar crystals can dissolve. Churn in an ice-cream machine. This can also be made without using an ice-cream machine. You can just place it in the freezer and keep on whisking it well every 30 minutes until it's nice and fluffy and frozen.

To make the berry compote, place the sugar, 50 ml (1¾ fl oz) of water and the orange zest in a small saucepan over medium heat and stir to dissolve the sugar. Bring up to the boil, then set aside to cool. Remove the orange zest.

Place all the berries in a bowl, add the sugar syrup and mix to combine. Spoon into small glasses or bowls, top with a small scoop of yoghurt gelato and add a mint leaf and serve.

An elegant and lovely dish to serve to your family and friends
— you can substitute the peach for any other fruit in season, such
as berries, mango, cherries, pear or whatever takes your fancy.

peach jelly with vanilla bean panna cotta

MAKES 20

To make the panna cotta, place the double and single cream, sugar and vanilla in a saucepan over medium heat, stir to dissolve the sugar and bring to the boil. Soak the gelatine in cold water until softened, squeeze to remove any excess liquid then whisk into the cream mixture. Strain and cool to room temperature.

Pour some of the cooled panna cotta into 20 small glasses. Refrigerate for 1 hour or until set.

To make the peach jelly, place the peach, sugar and 250 ml (9 fl oz/1 cup) of water in a saucepan over medium heat. Stir to dissolve the sugar and bring to the boil. Strain and discard the peach. Soak the gelatine in cold water until soft and squeeze to remove any excess liquid then whisk into the mixture. Cool to room temperature.

Pour a thin layer of the peach jelly on top of the panna cotta and refrigerate for 1 hour or until set.

Add the diced peaches to the remaining jelly (you might need to gently heat it again and cool) and gently mix.

Remove the glasses from the refrigerator, place a teaspoon of the diced peaches on top of each, then top with some mint and serve.

1 peach, finely diced
small mint sprigs, to serve

panna cotta
225 g (8 oz) double cream
225 ml (7¾ oz) single cream
70 g (2½ oz) caster (superfine) sugar
1 vanilla bean, split lengthways and
    seeds scraped
2½ x 2 g gold gelatine leaves

peach jelly
2 peaches, chopped
180 g (6 oz) caster (superfine) sugar
2 x 2 g gold gelatine leaves

gin iced tea

SERVES 4

Place all the ingredients except the tonic water into a carafe. Serve into cups over ice and top up each cup with tonic water and garnish with the apple crisps.

180 ml (6 fl oz) gin (Hendrick's works well)
60 ml (2 fl oz/¼ cup) Cointreau
3 dashes of orange bitters
120 ml (4 fl oz) ruby red grapefruit juice
60 ml (2 fl oz/¼ cup) grapefruit juice
40 ml (1¼ fl oz) tonic water
4 apple crisps, to garnish (Gala apples
   work well) (see page 241)

kentucky ice tea

SERVES 1

Build all the ingredients in a glass over ice and garnish with a tea flower.

45 ml (1½ fl oz) Bourbon
100 ml (3½ fl oz) clear apple juice
5 ml (1 teaspoon) black tea sugar syrup
   (see page 239)
8 mint leaves
tea flower, to garnish

espresso chilli martini

SERVES 1

2 orange zests
orange wedge
chilli sugar (see page 242)
45 ml (1½ fl oz) Cognac
5 ml (1 teaspoon) Grand Marnier
30 ml (1 fl oz) fresh espresso shot
5 ml (1 teaspoon) Toussaint coffee liqueur
10 ml (½ fl oz) maple and chilli syrup
    (see page 238)
3 coffee beans, to garnish

Stain a martini glass with orange zests. Use the orange wedge to run around the rim of the glass, then dip half of the rim of the glass into the chilli sugar. Place the remaining ingredients in a shaker over ice and shake vigorously. Strain into the martini glass and add the coffee beans for 'health, wealth and happiness'.

berry iced tea

SERVES 1

45 ml (1½ fl oz) vodka
45 ml (1½ fl oz) berry tea, freshly made and
    cooled to room temperature
30 ml (1 fl oz) cranberry juice
dash of sugar syrup
5 raspberries
5 blackberries
10 ml (2 teaspoons) lemon juice
15 ml (½ fl oz) elderflower cordial
fresh raspberries and blueberries,
    to garnish

Place the ingredients in a shaker and shake over ice, then strain into a highball glass over crushed ice. Garnish with fresh raspberries and blueberries.

white chocolate martini

SERVES 1

Place all the ingredients in a shaker over ice. Shake and then fine strain into a martini glass and garnish with the marbled chocolate shard.

NOTE: To make the marbled chocolate shard, melt 100 g (3½ oz) dark chocolate (70% cocoa) in a bowl over a saucepan of simmering water. Melt 50 g (1¾ oz) white chocolate in a bowl over a saucepan of simmering water. Line 2 baking trays with 2 pieces of acetate. Drizzle over the dark chocolate then drizzle over the white chocolate. Using a spatula, spread the chocolate to 1 mm thick creating a marbled effect. Cool slightly, then score into large squares. Refrigerate to set.

45 ml (1½ fl oz) vodka
30 ml (1 fl oz) white crème de cacao
(white chocolate liqueur)
dash of sugar syrup (see page 238)
large marbled chocolate shard, to garnish
(see note)

berry royale

SERVES 1

Place the crème de framboise, Chambord, grapefruit and lemon juice in a Champagne flute. Top with Champagne and garnish with skewered raspberries and blueberries.

10 ml (2 teaspoons) crème de framboise
(raspberry liqueur)
5 ml (1 teaspoon) Chambord (French black
raspberry liqueur)
30 ml (1 fl oz) ruby red grapefruit juice
5 ml (1 teaspoon) lemon juice
Champagne
skewered fresh raspberries and
blueberries, to garnish

mediterranean royale

SERVES 1

1 white sugar cube
3 dashes of orange bitters
1 lemon zest
15 ml (½ fl oz) Aperol
sparkling rosé wine
candied orange slice, to garnish
    (see page 241)

Soak the sugar cube with the orange bitters and drop into a champagne glass. Stain the glass with the lemon zest, then discard the zest. Add the Aperol and top with the sparkling rosé and the candied orange slice to serve.

pomegranate royale

SERVES 1

30 ml (1 fl oz) Pama Liqueur
    (pomegranate liqueur)
5 ml (1 teaspoon) lemon juice
dash of rhubarb bitters
topped with sparkling wine
pomegranate seeds, to garnish

Place all the ingredients in a shaker except the sparkling wine, roll and then strain into a champagne glass. Top with the sparkling wine and garnish with the pomegranate seeds.

basics

spirits

Spirits are essentially grain, vegetable or fruit fermented with sugar and yeast to create alcohol. The 'mash' is then distilled to create the spirit that gets filtered and either blended with water in the bottle (vodka) or aged and then blended with water and added to the bottle (any dark spirit). All dark spirits start their life as translucent liquids before being added to the barrel for ageing, where they pick up characteristics in colour and aroma from charred barrels or pre-aged barrels (Port, sherry or rum) before they are bottled.

vodka: pure and citrus

Vodka is not made solely from potatoes – sorry to break the myth! Nowadays drinkers are becoming more aware and you can drink to your dietary requirements if you're wheat intolerant by choosing rye-based vodka (Belvedere).

Essentially vodka is a grain or vegetal-based spirit that is distilled and mixed with water. Where the bottle details that a spirit is 40% ABV (alcohol by volume) the rest of the bottle is water – in some cases water that has been run over Champagne limestone (Grey Goose) or collected from a water source with AA purity (42 Below).

gin: london dry and plymouth

Gin is flavoured vodka – it is a neutral grain spirit that is distilled with botanicals (flavouring agents) that are washed over the spirit and then the spirit is distilled one more time before adding water and bottling.

There are different styles of modern gin – London Dry (made by distilling the neutral grain spirit with the heavy presence of citrus botanicals and stipulated that no sugars are added to the spirit and the distillate is only finished with water), Plymouth (made in the region of Plymouth), Old Tom (gin with added sugar) and Genève (aged gin).

Gin is also highly medicinal and is not a depressant. The quinine in tonic water is actually the depressant and was added to soda water in India for the British army to fight malaria (hence the name 'Indian Tonic water'). When they added the quinine to the soda water they renamed the potion 'tonic' and the gin and tonic came into being.

rum: white, golden, aged and dark

Rum is made from a sugar cane by-product called molasses. It is essentially pressed from the sugar cane, fermented to make alcohol and then distilled and bottled (white rum) or distilled and aged in barrels (primarily oak) to create golden, aged and dark rum.

tequila: blanco, reposado, anejo and mezcal

Tequila is made from the blue agave plant – a member of the lily family. Tequila has five varietals; blanco, joven, reposado, anejo and extra anejo from 51% agave to 100% agave. To be an official Tequila, it must be made in the state of Jalisco, Mexico.

Blanco: 'Silver' un-aged or bottled directly after distillation or aged in stainless steel barrels or unoaked barrels for less than two months.

Joven: 'Young' or gold is created based on blending Blanco and reposado or anejo Tequila.

Reposado: 'Rested' is aged a minimum of two months but less than one year in oak barrels.

Anejo: 'Aged' for a minimum of one year but less than three years.

Extra Anejo: 'Extra Aged' aged a minimum of three years in oak barrels.

Mezcal: A regional variety of Tequila, made in Oaxaca from an agave called maguey. Mezcal has a distinct smoky flavour compared to tequila, made from the blue agave plant.

bourbon

Bourbon is an American whiskey that has to be at least 51% corn (with most around 70% corn and a mix of wheat and rye) and is named after the county of Bourbon, Kentucky. In 1964 a law was passed that acknowledged bourbon as a 'distinctive product of the United States'.

The ageing process of bourbon stipulates that no artificial colour or flavour can be added and it is to be aged in new charred oak barrels, where the aromas and characteristics are picked up from the barrel. Most bourbons are released from the barrel and then diluted to make a minimum of 40% ABV but some are 'barrel proof' and bottled straight from the barrel.

single malt whisky

Single malt is a whisky distilled from barley (sometimes rye) created from a single distillery. Most single malt whiskies come from Scotland (with some from Ireland and Japan) where they are determined by the five regions: Highlands, Lowlands, Islay, Speyside and Campbeltown. Scottish, Irish and Japanese Whiskies omit the 'e' in their spelling.

blended whisky

Blended whisky is when multiple whiskies such as single malt and grain whiskies are blended together. If single malt whiskies are mixed together, then it is called a 'vatted' whisky.

cognac

Cognac is fine French brandy (eau de vie). It is double-distilled in pot stills in the Cognac region. The distilled grapes are sourced from the region of Cognac.

Armagnac was one of the first French brandies single distilled in column stills with the grapes sourced from the region of Armagnac.

French brandies are aged as follows:

AC: Aged at least two years in wood

VS: 'Very Special' aged at least three years in wood

VSOP: 'Very Superior Old Pale' aged at least 5 years in wood

XO: 'Extra Old' aged at least six years in wood

Hors d'age: The youngest brandy in this blend spends at least 10 years in wood.

Aperitif: An alcoholic beverage served pre dinner that stimulates the appetite.

Digestif: An alcoholic beverage served post dinner that aids digestion.

Liqueur: An alcoholic beverage that has been flavoured with fruit, herbs, spiced nuts or flowers with added sugars

Bitters: An alcoholic beverage that contains herbal essence and is a bitter or bittersweet flavour. Bitters were traditionally used as a digestif, their primary role now is as a contemporary cocktail flavouring agent.

Cordials: A non-alcoholic sweet fruit flavour which is primarily diluted with water, tonic or lemonade.

syrups and juice

sugar syrup

MAKES 400 ML (14 FL OZ)

Place the water and sugar in a small saucepan over low heat and stir until the sugar has dissolved. Increase the heat and simmer until the liquid is clear. Remove from the heat, set aside to cool, then bottle. Date your bottle and refrigerate until use.

250 ml (9 fl oz/1 cup) water
250 g (9 oz) white sugar or 250 g (9 oz) brown sugar for dark spirits

maple and chilli syrup

MAKES 300 ML (10½ FL OZ)

Place the water and maple syrup in a small saucepan over low heat and stir until the syrup has diluted. Then add the chilli and leave on the heat for 5 minutes. Remove from the heat and let it sit for 1 hour allowing the flavours to infuse. Once the syrup has cooled, strain, discarding the chilli and bottle. Date your bottle and refrigerate until use.

100 ml (3½ fl oz) water
250 g (9 oz) maple syrup
3 whole chillies

honey water

MAKES 500 ML (14 FL OZ)

Add the honey to the warm sugar syrup and stir thoroughly to dilute.

200 g (7 oz) honey
400 ml (14 fl oz) warm sugar syrup

homemade falernum

MAKES 250 ML (9 FL OZ)

Place the orgeat syrup in a small saucepan, then add the vanilla. Warm over low heat to infuse the flavour for 5 minutes, then take off the heat and let sit to infuse. Add the Angostura bitters and lime juice and stir together. Once the syrup has cooled strain, discard the vanilla bean. Date your bottle and refrigerate.

200 ml (7 fl oz) orgeat syrup
  (almond syrup)
2 vanilla beans, split and seeds scraped
10 ml (2 teaspoons) Angostura bitters
50 ml (1½ fl oz) lime juice

fruit or herb sugar syrup variations

MAKES 400 ML (14 FL OZ)

250 ml (9 fl oz/1 cup) water
250 g (9 fl oz) white sugar or 250 g
   (9 fl oz) brown sugar for dark spirits

Place the water and sugar in a small saucepan over low heat and stir until the sugar has dissolved. Increase the heat and simmer until the liquid is clear. Remove from the heat, add the fruit, herb or spice, bring it back to a simmer for 5 minutes to warm the fruit/spices and then remove from the heat and let it sit for 1 hour to allow the flavours to infuse. Once the syrup has cooled, strain and discard the fruit, herb or spice and bottle. Date your bottle and refrigerate until use.

raspberry syrup – add 12 fresh raspberries.
ginger syrup – add 10 large slices of ginger.
lemongrass syrup – add 3 x 10 cm (4 inch) long lemongrass stems, bruising them as you add them to the syrup.
saffron and honey syrup – add 5 saffron threads and reduce the sugar to 150 g (5½ oz) based on 100 g (3½ oz) of honey being added.
spiced apricot and vanilla syrup – add 8 dried apricots cut in half, 2 star anise with 2 split and scraped vanilla beans.
spiced syrup – add 4 cinnamon sticks, 2 star anise, 2 cloves and 1 whole nutmeg.
ginger and orange syrup – add 6 large slices of ginger with the zest from 3 large oranges.
vanilla syrup – add 4 split and scraped vanilla beans.
lime zest syrup – add the zest from 5 limes.
black tea sugar syrup – add 3 teaspoons black tea leaves to the warm syrup and let it sit for 15 minutes only and then strain.

seasonal fruit purée

MAKES 200 G (7 OZ) PURÉE

75 ml (2¼ fl oz) water
75 g (2½ oz) sugar
200 g (7 oz) prepared seasonal fruit
   (see below right)

Place the water and sugar in a small saucepan over low heat and stir until the sugar has dissolved. Add the fruit, increase the heat and gently simmer until the fruit softens. Then place all the fruit and liquid in a blender. Once blended, strain through a fine sieve to remove any pulp. Date your bottle and refrigerate until ready to use.

strawberry purée – remove the stalks and slice in half.
peach purée – blanch and remove the skin from ripe peaches. Cut into slices and then cut into 2 cm (¾ inch) pieces.
cherry purée – remove the stalk and cut a slice into the fruit. Once the cherries have been simmered, remove the seed from the pulp before placing in the blender.
pear purée – peel and core ripe pears and then cut into 2 cm (¾ inch) pieces.

fruit crisps

MAKES 12

1 large granny smith apple, pear, pineapple,
   peach or mango, thinly sliced
(see note for detail for orange)
60 ml (2 fl oz/¼ cup) sugar syrup

Preheat the oven to 90°C (195°F/Gas ½). Slice the fruit on a mandolin or with a very sharp knife to create slices 1–2 mm (⅟₁₆ inch) thickness. Lay them onto a tray lined with an ovenproof silicone mat, and then brush them with the sugar syrup on both sides and place into the oven or 2–3 hours. Keeping an eye on the fruit, once they are lightly brown, then take out of the oven and allow to cool completely. Place into airtight containers with non-stick baking paper between the layers to ensure they don't stick, add moisture absorbing beads to ensure they stay dry.

This can work for any fruit with a matted texture and is a simple way to dress your drinks and impress your guests.

NOTE: For candied slices of oranges and cumquats, thinly slice as above, then sit the fruit in sugar syrup for 30 minutes prior to putting into the oven. Cook at 90°C (220°F/Gas ½) for 2 hours.

candied chilli

SERVES 4

1 large red chilli
100 ml (3½ fl oz) sugar syrup

Preheat the oven to 120°C (250°F/Gas 1). Slice the chilli lengthways with a very sharp knife to create 4 even quarters and remove the seeds. Bring the sugar syrup to a simmer and put the quarters into the syrup on the heat for 5 minutes. Then take the chilli quarters out of the syrup and place onto a baking tray lined with an ovenproof silicone mat. Cook for 8 minutes and then take out of the oven and let them cool to crisp.

signature salt

MAKES ABOUT 100 G (3½ OZ)

100 g (3½ oz) sea salt
   (Maldon sea salt works well)
Add the finely grated zest from 6 limes
   (or other citrus fruit) or 50 g (1¾ oz)
   of spice
pinch of dry rice grains

Place the sea salt and zest in a completely dry small dish, add a pinch of rice grains and seal with plastic wrap. Date and leave in a dry place above the oven or in a warm dry room for 24 hours to infuse the salt.

Remove the plastic wrap and taste to ensure the flavour has infused the salt. Check that the salt is still dry and then remove the zest. Leave the rice grains in the salt as they absorb any moisture. Store in an airtight container.

signature sugars

MAKES ABOUT 100 G (3½ OZ)

100 g (3½ oz) sugar
fruit zest, spice or herb
pinch of dry rice grains

Place the sugar and fruit zest, spice or herb in a completely dry small dish, add a large pinch of rice grains and seal with plastic wrap. Date and leave in a dry place above the oven or in a warm dry room for 48 hours to infuse the sugar.

Remove the plastic wrap and taste to ensure the flavour has infused the sugar and it is still dry. Remove the zest, spice or herbs, leave the rice grains in the sugar as they absorb any moisture. Store in an airtight container.

chilli sugar – add 25 g (1 oz) chilli flakes or ground chilli powder to the sugar.
lemon sugar – add the finely grated zest from 3 lemons to the sugar.
vanilla sugar – add 2 vanilla beans cut into 4 with the seeds scraped out placed into the sugar.
orange sugar – add the finely grated zest of 3 large oranges in the sugar.
cinnamon sugar – add 25 g (1 oz) of ground cinnamon and blend with the sugar.
coconut sugar – add 100 g (3½ oz) desiccated coconut in a bowl with the sugar.

flaming

CITRUS FRUITS WORK BEST DUE TO THE OILS IN THE SKIN

large fruit zests cut to measure 3 x 6 cm
(1¼ x 2½ inch)

Cut large pieces of zest about 3 cm (1¼ inches) wide by 6 cm (2½ inches) long from a fresh, hard fruit with only a thin layer of pith attached so you have a thicker piece making it easier to hold. To flame the zests do each one at a time. Hold the zest between your thumb and index finger with the outer skin of the zest facing away from your palm. Warm the zest with a naked flame for 3 seconds and when you're ready hold the zest over the inside of the glass with the naked flame and squeeze the zest to release the fruit essence to flame – a flame will burst for 1 second from the zest. Discard the zest once it has flamed.

homemade brews

homemade ginger beer

MAKES 1 LITRE (35 FL OZ/4 CUPS)

Place all the ingredients into a container and seal it. Let it sit for 24 hours to macerate at room temperature. When you open it, discard any film from the top and then fine strain. Pour into a bottle, seal and date, and refrigerate until use.

1 litre (35 fl oz/4 cups) boiling water
200 g (7 oz) white sugar
50 ml (1¾ fl oz) lemon juice
1 tablespoon of ground ginger
6 thin slices ginger
1 teaspoon dried yeast
250 ml (9 fl oz/1 cup) sparkling mineral
    water (optional)

lemonade

MAKES 1½ LITRES (52 FL OZ/6 CUPS)

Place the sugar, lemon juice, lemon myrtle and lemongrass into a saucepan and bring to a simmer for 5 minutes. Once the sugar has dissolved, let it sit for 1 hour and then strain all ingredients off and set aside to cool. Pour into a bottle with the mineral water, seal and date, and refrigerate until use.

300 g (10½ oz) white sugar
350 ml (12 fl oz) lemon juice
3 leaves lemon myrtle
2 x 10 cm (4 inch) lemongrass stems
1 litre (35 fl oz/4 cups) sparkling
    mineral water

essence of jasmine green tea

MAKES 115 ML (3¾ FL OZ)

Add half the jasmine green tea leaves to a cup and then top with hot water. Leave it to steep for 2 hours and then strain the tea off and retain the jasmine tea dilution. Then add the remaining tea leaves with the jasmine tea dilution to a saucepan and bring to a simmer for 5 minutes before taking it off the heat to steep for another hour. Once steeped strain the tea off and add the sugar syrup before bottling.

30 g (1 oz) loose jasmine green leaf tea
150 ml (5 fl oz) hot water
15 ml (½ fl oz) sugar syrup

jellies and foams

gin and tonic jelly

MAKES 16 PIECES

120 ml (4 fl oz) gin (Plymouth Gin
    works well)
30 ml (1 fl oz) sugar syrup
6 pieces of orange zest (6 x 3 cm
    x 6 cm /1¼ x 2½ inch)
    pieces orange zest
8 x 2 g gold gelatine leaves
360 ml (12½ fl oz) tonic water, chilled

Warm the gin and sugar syrup with the orange zests in a small saucepan over low heat for 5 minutes (it is important the liquid doesn't boil). Soften the gelatine leaves in cold water. Then squeeze to remove any excess water and add to the warm liquid, stirring to dissolve. Set aside to cool for 10 minutes. Add the cold tonic water and pour into a 13 x 13 cm (5 x 5 inch) tray lined with plastic wrap, skimming off any froth. Refrigerate for 2 hours or until set. Carefully lift out of tray and place on a flat surface and cut with a very sharp knife into 3 cm (1¼ inch) squares.

NOTE: You can set them in small shot glasses if you prefer. Vodka, lemon and basil or Champagne and orange can be used as variations.

sauternes jelly

MAKES 16 PIECES

280 ml (9½ fl oz) sauternes
30 ml (1 fl oz) sugar syrup
3 pieces of lemon zest (3 x 3 cm
    x 6 cm/1¼ x 2½ inch)
8 x 2 g gold gelatine sheets

Warm half of the sauternes with the sugar syrup and lemon zests in a small saucepan over low heat for 5 minutes (it is important the liquid doesn't boil). Soften the gelatine leaves in cold water, then squeeze to remove any excess water and add to the warm liquid, stirring to dissolve. Set aside to cool for 10 minutes. Add the cold sauternes and pour into a 13 x 13 cm (5 x 5 inch) tray lined with plastic wrap. Refrigerate for 2 hours or until set. Carefully lift out of the tray and place on a flat surface and cut with a very sharp knife into 3 cm (1¼ inch) squares.

NOTE: You can set them in small shot glasses if you prefer.

elderflower foam

MAKES 10 DRINKS

200 ml (7 fl oz) elderflower cordial
50 ml (1¾ fl oz) sugar syrup
100 ml (3½ fl oz) egg white

Place all the ingredients in a cream canister and seal tightly. Add the gas bulb to the canister. Shake the canister thoroughly for 3 minutes and then place the canister into the refrigerator for approximately 2 hours or in the freezer for 30 minutes. The key to any foam is to chill it prior to serving. Once the canister is chilled, shake and test it for consistency. Once you know the foam is ready, place on the top of the surface of the drink and ease the gas gun to squirt the foam into the drink surface. When you have finished using the foam, place it back into the refrigerator and date — you shouldn't keep for more than 4 days.

VARIATION: You could make this foam using clear apple or cranberry juice instead of elderflower cordial.

tailored ice

ice spheres

The easiest way to make home ice spheres is to buy small party balloons and fill them with cooled, boiled water. The reason you use boiled water is to reduce the oxygen content which ensures the ice comes out clear. If it's hard to fill the balloons, you can place a balloon over the nozzle of a tap and fill from there, then place straight into the freezer. Ideally, you want to tie a knot at the base of the balloon neck, so you freeze an almost perfect circular shape. These can be stored and used when you're ready. I always keep 4 or 5 in the freezer for that unknown moment of entertainment.

VARIATION: For 500 ml (17 fl oz/2 cups) of water, add 3 split and scraped vanilla beans when boiling the water and then fine strain and use as above.

ice blocks

Depending on how much room you have in your freezer, take a very clean small to medium oven tray with deep sides and fill with cooled, boiled water. Once it is frozen, you can pop it out of the tray and position on the table next to the rare spirits selection for chipped ice shards at the end of dinner. You will need an ice pick for this, and it is a simple, yet very cost effective piece of entertainment for the end of the night. You won't look at ice in the same way again.

equipment

Boston shaker – this consists of a metal tin and glass. At times the glass element of the Boston shaker is referred to as the mixing glass or shaker.

Strainers – Hawthorn: used when using the metal Boston. Julep: used when using only the glass Boston. Fine: used only when disregarding the fruit pulp.

Muddler – this is a flat-end utensil used to crush solid fruit or herbs and sugar.

Pitcher – a large glass jug used to make martinis. Traditional pitchers have a straining lip.

Glassware – Old fashioned, martini and highball are essential. A coupette glass is an elegant option similar to a martini glass.

methodologies

Shake – a standard shake is when you join the steel Boston from the bench top with the glass Boston from the top, tap the two together to seal and then shake the cubed ice and liquid.

Vigorously shake – a vigorous shake is when you seal the Bostons together and then you shake it hard throwing the ice and liquid from steel to glass in the Bostons for a prolonged period of time. This is typically used when you want to emulsify egg white in a drink.

Roll – a roll is when you hold the two Bostons together with a light seal and no ice and you literally roll the liquid from one Boston to the other gently bringing the liquid together. This method is typically used when you want to you want to maintain the texture – for example, a bloody mary or thick juice.

Zest – this is when you cut a zest from the fruit skin and retain the skin without the pith. If you do cut the zest with pith then you can use a sharp knife to take the pith off the skin afterwards.

Fine strain – this is when you use the double strainer (tea strainer) to pour the liquid into the glass. It is typically used when you want to strain the fruit pulp or herbs from a drink after shaking.

Stain – this is when you twist a citrus fruit zest into the glass to release the essence from the skin. Discard the zest after use.

Bruise – press the herb in the glass to release flavours. You should only press six times with a flat end against a glass.

acknowledgements

This has been my most enjoyable book to work on and I also know the team that put it together loved coming to work when we were shooting — we basically had our own small party each day with delicious food and drinks.

The people I would like to thank are:

Juliet Rogers and Kay Scarlett — the head honchos that continue to bat for me.

Jane Lawson, Livia Caiazzo and Sonia Greig for the countless emails to make sure it all makes sense. Reuben Crossman for designing yet another wonderful book that could possibly win you another award to put in your pool room.

Anson Smart (photographer) and David Morgan (stylist) — boys our third book together and each one looks better than the last... Thank you once again, you guys rock! A big thank you to Monica and Jacinta Cannataci (the wonder twins) for preparing all the food and testing the recipes in the kitchen. Kim Lockyer, for your commitment on this project — you are a star! All my staff past, present and future that I have had the joy of working with and learning from over the years at Hugos, The Pantry and on catering jobs — love your work guys!

Once again, thank you to my business partners Dave Evans, Dave Corsi, Daniel Vaughan, Guy Mainwaring and Daddy'O for allowing me the room to grow as a chef. A big thanks to John Pye for helping me understand South American flavours. Mark Ward for his utterly delicious cocktails — you, brother, are a very naughty man when you make me cocktails — but I love ya!

And lastly, my family — Mum, Astrid, Udo, Leonie, Walter and Poldi for your ongoing support, and to Chilli and Indii, my beautiful daughters, you make me smile all day, every day.

This book is dedicated to all my readers out there — as I have said before, if you take just one recipe (and perhaps one cocktail) and incorporate it into your cooking repertoire then I know this book has been well worth it.

Cheers, Pete

index

Published in 2010 by Murdoch Books Pty Limited

Murdoch Books Australia
Pier 8/9
23 Hickson Road
Millers Point NSW 2000
Phone: +61 (0) 2 8220 2000
Fax: +61 (0) 2 8220 2558
www.murdochbooks.com.au

Murdoch Books UK Limited
Erico House, 6th Floor
93–99 Upper Richmond Road
Putney, London SW15 2TG
Phone: +44 (0) 20 8785 5995
Fax: +44 (0) 20 8785 5985
www.murdochbooks.co.uk

Publisher: Kay Scarlett
Designer: Reuben Crossman
Photographer: Anson Smart
Stylist: David Morgan
Project Manager: Livia Caiazzo
Food Editor: Sonia Greig
Production Controller: Kita George

Murdoch Books and the stylist would like to thank:
DeDeCe www.dedeceplus.com
Shelley Panton www.shelleypanton.com
Mud Australia www.mudaustralia.com
Wasara www.wasara.jp

National Library of Australia Cataloguing-in-Publication Data

Author: Evans, Pete.
Title: My party / Pete Evans.
ISBN: 9781741968163 (hbk.)
Notes: Includes index.
Subjects: Cocktails.
         Appetisers.
         Cookery.
         Entertaining
         Cocktail parties.
         Parties.

Dewey Number: 641.568
A catalogue record for this book is available from the
British Library.

PRINTED BY 1010 PRINTING INTERNATIONAL LIMITED, CHINA

IMPORTANT: Those who might be at risk from the effects
of salmonella poisoning (the elderly, pregnant women,
young children and those suffering from immune deficiency
diseases) should consult their doctor with any concerns about
eating raw eggs.

OVEN GUIDE: You may find cooking times vary depending on
the oven you are using. For fan-forced ovens, as a general rule,
set the oven temperature to 20°C (35°F) lower than indicated
in the recipe.

OTHER TITLES BY PETE EVANS:

fish

Fish follows on from Pete's successful television series of the same name. The book focuses on Australian seafood as an accessible, easy and delicious starting point for any meal. Recipes are divided by type of fish, listed in easy-to-use alphabetical order, with suggested alternatives given for each recipe. *Fish* also includes a wealth of information on Australian seafood, its health benefits, history and future.

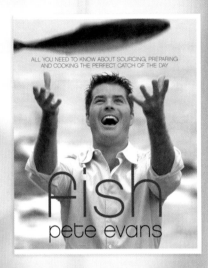

my table

Chef and restaurateur Pete Evans believes entertaining should be as much fun for the cook as for the guests around the table. Here he share his menus and secrets for casual entertaining. *My Table* is the antithesis of restaurant dining and aims to minimise the time the host spends in the kitchen. Pete caters for indoor and outdoor dining with recipes for all seasons and moods, from a very special prawn sandwich to a wintry roast dinner. There's a stylish selection of drinks to set the scene and simple desserts to finish. *My Table* will encourage even the most reluctant cook to share good food, simply prepared, with family and friends.

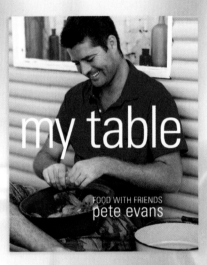

my grill

Chef, restaurateur and TV presenter Pete Evans is fired up about a subject very close to his, and every man's, heart – the barbecue. Tongs in hand, Pete takes you through three chapters of sizzling recipes starting with a weekend away, through to a lazy afternoon barbecue and finishing with a more stylish evening affair. The recipes are beautifully illustrated and range from simple dishes like baked eggs with chorizo to a light Thai beef salad and a scrumptious parmesan and sage crusted pork cutlet with fennel salad. Each chapter also contains cocktails to add fuel to the fire.

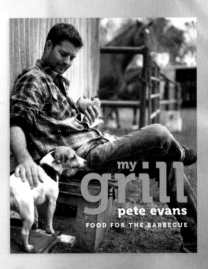